W9-ANK-136

I Want to See You, Lord

Anne Ortlund

HARVEST HOUSE PUBLISHERS
Eugene, Oregon 97402

Cover design by Koechel-Peterson & Associates, Minneapolis, Minnesota

I WANT TO SEE YOU, LORD

Copyright © 1998 by Anne Ortlund
Published by Harvest House Publishers
Eugene, Oregon 97402

Ortlund, Anne.
    [Fix your eyes on Jesus]
    I want to see you, Lord / Anne Ortlund.
      p. cm.
    Originally published: Fix your eyes on Jesus. Dallas : Word Pub., © 1991.
    Includes bibliographical references.
    ISBN 1-56507-816-0
    1. Christian life.   2. Jesus Christ—Example.   3. Jesus Christ—Influence.
  4. Ortlund, Anne. I. Title.
    [BV4501.2.O726   1998]
    248.4—DC21

                                                     97-36914
                                                      CIP

Printed in the United States of America.

98 99 00 01 02 03 04 / DC / 10 9 8 7 6 5 4 3 2 1

To Ray

husband

lover

coach

model

shaper

cheering section

pastor

leader

inspirer

confidante

counselor

playmate

best friend

co-laborer in the gospel

*one whose very life urges me to
keep my eyes on Jesus*

Contents

PART 5: LOOKING TO JESUS FOR A CLEAR FOCUS

PART 6: LOOKING TO JESUS NOW AND ALWAYS

It's the look that saves,
but it's the gaze that sanctifies.

Jesus

Where Is Our Focus?

I was chatting last Sunday with my in-laws; they're dear people. We covered this and that, and got to discussing a particular pastor. Oh, so subtly, so delicately, I managed to allude to his struggles, perils, possible problems. . . . I rattled on. . . .

Suddenly I saw myself—fangs, claws, and all.

I was making sure they understood that Ray and I never had such struggles, perils, possible problems—that we must obviously be superior. I was too well-bred to say it; I only inferred it. My relatives are savvy people; they'd understand.

The Spirit stopped me cold.

My eyes weren't on Jesus, they were on my family—to make sure Ray and I looked good in their sight. That gave freedom to my "old nature" (my familiar, ugly, life-long enemy) to take control of my tongue, and there in front of all of them was my exposed heart, with all its lurking pride and jealousy.

Embarrassing! Discouraging!

I apologized, and my sweet family made light of it and of course forgave me.

Perhaps you've found yourself in that spot, too. It seems as if we're always just one step from disaster, doesn't it? And there's no help, no winning, unless we follow Hebrews 12:2—fix our eyes on Jesus, one moment at a time.

Do you need this book? I do. Let's learn from it and obey what it says together.

PART ONE

Looking
to Jesus Alone

*W*hat does it take," someone asked a circus tightrope walker, "to do what you do?"

"Three things," he answered.

"Raw courage. You commit yourself to begin walking, and then you can't change your mind.

"Balance. You can't lean too far this way or that.

"Most of all, concentration. You fix your eyes on that wire, and until it's all over you never shift your attention."

He paused. Then—

"Never," he said firmly.

Jesus

An Invitation from Jesus

When the Israelites were traveling in the desert, there was a time when they had gotten into so much sin that God sent snakes among them to bite them, and many died. But then God said to Moses,

> "Make a snake and put it up on a pole; anyone who is bitten can look at it and live." So Moses made a bronze snake and put it on a pole. Then when anyone was bitten by a snake and looked at the bronze snake, he lived (Numbers 21:8-9).

And Jesus—the final, ultimate healer—told Nicodemus,

> Just as Moses lifted up the snake in the desert, so the Son of Man must be lifted

up, that everyone who believes in him may
have eternal life (John 3:14-15).

But does Jesus, lifted up, seem too remote? Or
does He intimidate you? I'm praying as I write that
you'll understand just how personable He is.

"Come to me," He says (Matthew 11:28).

"Handle me, and see" (Luke 24:39 KJV).

How tender He is, how unthreatening! He's
wooing you, saying, "Don't be afraid; just believe"
(Mark 5:36).

> He does not fight or shout;
> He does not raise His voice!
> He does not crush the weak,
> Or quench the smallest hope
> (Matthew 12:19 TLB).

Paul tells us in 1 Timothy that God is on one side
and all the people on the other side, and Christ Jesus,
Himself man, is between them to bring them together
(TLB).

So come, my friend. *I* came many years ago. You
come, too.

> Let us draw near to God with a sincere
> heart in full assurance of faith, having our
> hearts sprinkled to cleanse us from a
> guilty conscience (Hebrews 10:22). For
> Christ . . . suffered for sins, the just for the
> unjust, that he might bring us to God
> (1 Peter 3:18 KJV).

For your personal salvation, what an "unspeakable gift" He is (2 Corinthians 9:15)! Or as the Living Bible says, a "Gift too wonderful for words."

Won't you look to Jesus…and see how wonderful He is?

A parting
Glance

There is no beauty
to be discovered anywhere
comparable to fixing your eyes on Jesus.

There is no life-changing power available
anywhere comparable to that gaze.

Giving Him Your Full Attention

I crawled into bed last night thinking about Ray's news that a fellow's going to do a few guest-speaker spots on Ray's "Haven of Rest" broadcast. Ray was still in the bathroom, but I called in loudly to him, "Did you tell him it's to renew and encourage believers? We don't want somebody ranting and raving over social issues and controversies. Does he understand 'Haven's' flavor?"

Ray came around the corner and got into bed. "Don't be such a fusser, Anne. Why are you fussing?"

We hugged each other and I bellowed in his ear, "What do you mean, fuss? I never fuss! It's totally contrary to my gentle, mellow nature to fuss!" And we laughed ourselves silly. (It's great living together after the kids are gone. You can scream and yell and do what you want.)

Of course we both knew my natural inclination *is* to fuss. I'm conscientious and meticulous and I'm always anticipating how to cover details. Though I've been a Christian for many years, I can still fuss; I can be really obnoxious. Then it's back to repenting and refocusing my eyes on Jesus—and I'm once more relaxed and happy.

You see, the Lord says to you and me continually, "Look unto me, and be ye saved...for I am God, and there is none else" (Isaiah 45:22 KJV).

I need constantly to be saved *from myself.* Do you? Do you need to be saved from

> your fears,
> your angers,
> your bad memories,
> your orneryness,
> your addictions,
> your temptations to escape instead of to conquer,
> your lusts,
> your depression,
> your laziness?

Says Hebrews 12:2, *"Let us fix our eyes on Jesus."*

In your attempts to save you from yourself, maybe you're more absorbed in looking at *people.* But God says, "Man ... is of few days and full of trouble....Like a fleeting shadow, he does not endure. Do you fix your eyes on such a one?" (Job 14:1-3).

No, no, we mustn't. "Lord," said Peter, "to whom else shall we go? You have the words of eternal life" (John 6:68).

Listen:

> Whether you aren't yet a Christian,
>> Or you're a new one,
>>> Or you've walked with Him a long time—

The only eternal, universal, triumphant, ever-contemporary Lord Jesus Christ (the One with the scars in His hands) commands, "Give Me your full attention. I Myself, and only I, hold the answers for every circumstance of your life. *Fix your eyes on Me.*"

PART TWO

Looking to Jesus
for Practical Help

*F*ix your eyes on Jesus as your Example, and be ashamed.

Fix your eyes on Jesus as your Savior, and be rescued.

Fix your eyes on Jesus as your Physician, and be made whole.

Fix your eyes on Jesus as your Mentor, and be taught.

Fix your eyes on Jesus as your Comforter, and be encouraged.

Fix your eyes on Jesus as your Strength, and be enabled.

Fix your eyes on Jesus as your Life, and live abundantly forever.

THREE

When You Have Too Much to Do

Ten months after Ray and I were married, we had baby Sherry.

Eleven and a half months later we had Margie.

Seventeen months later we had Buddy.

And immediately after that, Ray had a shrew for a wife.

My problem wasn't Ray or the babies; all four were adorable! My problem was no quiet time, no focus. My eyes weren't on Jesus, they were on what I had to do.

> A work-centered life gets complex, and it leads to burnout. A Christ-centered life—even in the midst of work—stays basically simple, nourished, and rested.

(When I got ornery enough to get desperate, I got back to Jesus again. Then little by little I didn't yell so much, and I guess Ray decided he could stick out being married to me after all.)

In looking back, I've learned from two weaknesses I have.

One, especially in earlier days, sometimes I wasn't really as busy as I *felt* I was busy. The pressure I put on myself kept "overheating my motor" and making me feel pushed.

Two, I tended to feel crowded periods before they ever arrived, and to be tired just from anticipating them.

You see, our actual living is between our ears. If you're unhappy or anxious over what's happening or what's going to happen, then you'll become tense and discouraged.

So don't keep your focus on your concerns. When I've done that it's made me fragmented and harried.

"Martha, Martha," the Lord said, "you are worried and upset about many things, but only one thing is needed. Mary has chosen what is better" (Luke 10:41-42).

Martha's problem wasn't cooking, it was the "many things." She was multidirectional, which always makes us feel oppressed, nervous, burdened, self-pitying, off-balance.

When your eyes are on Jesus, you begin to develop a reflex action inside you—it may take time—that shuns what's complicating, what's overwhelming.

You'll find you want to *do less* (but do the most important things) to *become more.*

Only then do you actually achieve more in your life. You'll find your life beginning to have wider-ranging and longer-lasting effects.

Focus your eyes on Jesus! Focus as Mary did; that's what I had to learn. Become a "one-thing" person (Luke 10:42).

How do you do this?

First, begin to develop the habit of continual fellowship with Him (see Chapter 17) in the midst of it all.

Second, determine to give Him the sacrifice of a regular "quiet time" (see Chapter 18). Yes, it will be a true sacrifice. ("You will never find time for anything," says Charles Bixton. "If you want time you must make it.")

Third, give Him frequent spaces when you momentarily quit, relax, breathe deeply, stretch your body, and say, "Jesus, my eyes are on You. You are able. You are helping me from one moment to the next. I trust You."

As you seek to do those three things and release control to Him, He will

> make the hours stretch,
> bring others to help you,
> cancel some things you thought you had to do,
> show you duties you can delegate,
> show you duties which don't have to be done
> at all.

I didn't learn my lesson once for all. I've had to come back over and over to take seriously again these practical words:

Reverence for God adds hours to each day.

(PROVERBS 10:27 TLB)

Let's pray together . . .

Lord Jesus, we accept your invitation in Matthew 11:29 to take Your yoke upon us. We want to learn from You—Creator, Producer, Worker, Achiever! Be our model, and teach us Your rhythm for living so that as we live, we'll find rest for our souls. In Your dear name, amen.

A parting
Glance

For the weariest day
May Christ be thy stay.
For the darkest night
May Christ be thy light.
For the weakest hour
May Christ be thy power.
For each moment's fall
May Christ be thy all.

—OLD BENEDICTION

FOUR

When You're Lonely

Have you moved recently and lost friends, leaving you feeling lonely?

Or have your friends moved and lost *you*, leaving you feeling lonely?

Or do you have people all around you yet you still feel lonely because they don't know you well, or worse, don't understand you?

Or are you a shut-in who knows all too well what it's like to be lonely?

Then turn your eyes to the only One who truly understands, because He's the only One who has ever experienced true loneliness.

Jesus wasn't totally abandoned and lonely when His own family thought He was crazy (Mark 3:21), or when all the people of His own hometown tried to kill Him (Luke 4:28-29). He wasn't totally lonely

- when His own fellow nationals took the responsibility for having Him crucified (Matthew 27:24-25),

- or when one of His own disciples turned Him in to make it happen (Matthew 26:14-16),

- or when His much-loved Peter denied any connection with Him (John 18:25-27),

- or even when eventually every one of His eleven best friends left Him in the lurch (Matthew 26:56).

Through it all He could turn to His Father for much-needed comfort and fellowship.

But then, for the first time in eternity, Jesus discovered true, ultimate loneliness. When He became sin for us (2 Corinthians 5:21), God Himself had to turn His face away and cut Him off.

Suddenly Jesus had no one at all—not even God!

In this new, strange, hellish horror, Jesus let loose a roar: "My God, my God, why have you forsaken me?" (Matthew 27:46).

> [It is] a scream of despairing agony in the darkness. It is the picture of an eclipsed God and a lost soul; it is the hour and power of darkness: the hosts of hell fill it, and the opaque sins of a world thicken it:

It is Jesus bearing MY sin in His own body
on the tree. It is Jesus taking the place of a
lost soul.[1]

*On the cross, Jesus became truly lonely so that you
and I would never need to be.*

Listen carefully: Your loneliness is unnecessary.
Do you know that?

In fact, if loneliness is long-term and chronic with
you, it's disobedient. It's not taking seriously His
promise, "Surely I am with you always" (Matthew
28:20).

You see, when on the cross Jesus found out what
real loneliness felt like, He made sure it need never
happen to you.

This is your secret to overcoming loneliness: Keep
your eyes on Him. People suggest lots of prescrip-
tions: get busy, get involved in your church and community, do things for others, find a friend, join a small
group—no, no!

First, in your loneliness, *draw from Jesus.* See how
He drew and drew from His Father, His ever-flowing
Source of all love and comfort and hope and pleasure
and fullness:

> Very early in the morning, when it was still
> dark, Jesus got up . . . [and] prayed (Mark
> 1:35).

He even deliberately sought aloneness for the best
togetherness of all:

> Crowds of people came to hear him. . . .
> But Jesus often withdrew to lonely places
> and prayed (Luke 5:15-16).

Have you done that lately? Have you sat at His feet and spread out your loneliness before Him? And admit that you've had your eyes focused on yourself.

Jesus is complete in the Father, and He says you are complete in Him (Colossians 2:9-10). He—and only He—is full of fullness for you. When, humanly speaking, you feel all alone, your heart can still be happy and satisfied: *You are complete in Him.*

> Though my father and mother forsake me,
> the Lord will receive me (Psalm 27:10).

Read the Bible; feast on it. Jesus is "Immanuel—which means, 'God with us'" (Matthew 1:23). He is closer than close, tender, comforting. He loves you! Drink in all that He is; He will become in you "a spring of water welling up to eternal life" (John 4:14).

Then in that fullness, go touch other lives. Get involved in your church and community, do things for others, find a friend, join a small group. . . .[2]

And wherever you go, you'll go in the spirit of satisfaction and wholeness and deep-welling joy—because first you were healed; first you turned your eyes upon Jesus.

Let's pray together...

O Lord Jesus, You know how cut off and lonely I've been feeling. Forgive me, Lord, for forgetting that my loneliness is unnecessary.

But now I come near to You, and according to Your promise in James 4:8, You have come near to me.

Lord, Psalm 16:8 says that in Your presence is fullness of joy! Thank You for making that possible.

Amen.

Strong are the walls around me
That hold me all the day,
But they who thus have bound me
Cannot keep God away.
My very prison walls are dear
Because the God I love is here.

They know, who thus oppress me
'Tis hard to be alone,
But know not, One can bless me
Who comes through bars and stone:
He makes my dungeon's darkness
   bright
And fills my bosom with delight.

— Madame Jeanne Guyon
   (1648-1717),
   written when she was in
   solitary confinement,
   because of her Christian
   faith, in a prison

When You're Sad

If you're feeling sad, there's a reason. Perhaps you've recently experienced some kind of loss. Studies indicate that depression—sadness—and loss go together.

- *Have you ever lost your wallet?* The sudden feeling in the pit of your stomach is depression.

- *Have you lost someone dear to you?* Your mourning is a form of depression.

- *Did you recently lose your job, or have you been demoted?* Your loss of status or earning a livelihood may lead to depression.

- *Are you wondering if people around you are thinking less of you?* Even an *imaginary* loss of status may produce depression.

- *Do your children fail to keep in touch, or refuse to respect you?* Your loss of relationship with them, as well as your very real loss of status as a parent, may bring depression.

- *Are you sick? Or are you worried that you might get sick?* A loss of health, or a possible projected loss of health, may bring depression.

- *Have you just finished a big project? Has there recently been a lot of excitement in your life?* A physical loss, even just a loss of adrenaline, may produce temporary depression until life becomes full again.

Maybe you can put your finger on why you're sad, maybe you can't. Either way, consider this: If your depression—your sadness—is longer than brief, it starts to become a dangerous enemy.

Many people don't realize what a threat sadness is—and any danger which is unrecognized as a danger is all the more dangerous. There is no stigma against sadness. There is no embarrassment, no alarm, no rushing to the Lord to eliminate it.

But God's Word says, "The joy of the LORD is your strength" (Nehemiah 8:10).

And when a Christian is sad—whether he realizes it or not, his power is diminished and he's vulnerable. It's been said that a country that has internal unrest is the least able to resist any threatening foreign power.

And a believer who is sad is the least able to resist any attack of Satan.

Depression is a sinister "fifth column" at work within the Christian community.

You watch a rejected congregation after a church split: As long as they're sad, there will be little true worship, little evangelism. The people can't focus on anything but themselves.

You watch an individual Christian who's sad: He's necessarily self-centered. As long as he's sad he—or she—makes a poor marriage partner.

When we're sad, we're sick. We don't function well. We don't lift and encourage other believers, and we don't appeal to unbelievers. Our spiritual strength and effectiveness are cut down.

No wonder the great George Mueller used to say, "My first business every morning is to make sure that my soul is happy in Jesus!"

Perhaps you're objecting. You're saying, "But Anne, things happen in our lives. Sometimes you can't put on a Pollyanna grin and chirp 'Praise the Lord' and pretend everything is wonderful."

You're absolutely right.

There *is* a time for tears:

- over sin and its resulting human misery (Matthew 5:4),

- in the burden of ministering to others (Acts 20:31),

- in compassion over the plights of others
  (Nehemiah 1:4; Romans 12:15),

and so on. . . .

In our living, we need to feel the full stretch of human emotions. When you need to cry—whether you're a man or a woman—let the tears flow and don't be ashamed.

When Lazarus died, *Jesus wept.*

Nevertheless, Jesus' very coming brought with it great power to comfort and be comforted—a great new capacity for deep, overcoming joy!

He came . . .

> To comfort all that mourn . . .
>> To give unto them beauty for ashes,
> the oil of joy for mourning,
>> the garment of praise for the spirit of
>>> heaviness.
>
> (ISAIAH 61:2-3 KJV)

He has taken away our susceptibility to a debilitating, long-term "spirit of heaviness."

"Do not let your hearts be troubled," He said (John 14:27). He wasn't saying, "There, there." He was saying, "Don't allow it! It's bad for you."

Paul was in prison facing death when he served as God's mouthpiece for this command: "Rejoice in the Lord" (Philippians 4:4).

That's not God's wish or His suggestion—it's His command. And it's for our best good. This command is so important that God had Paul say it twice:

"Rejoice in the Lord always. I will say it again: Rejoice!"

Maybe you're saying, "I am really sad these days. What can I do to get joy back in my life?"

Let me suggest a daily program for you to work on it:

1. Sit down before the Lord. Settle your mind in repose and calm.

2. Ask the Lord, "What are the knots in my tangledness—the specific situations in my life—that are giving me sadness?" Ask Him to put them in your mind; then write them in a list.

3. Now study slowly and carefully Philippians 4:6-7:

> Do not be anxious about anything, but in everything, by prayer and petition, with thanksgiving, present your requests to God [one knot—one item on your list—at a time].
>
> And the peace of God, which transcends all understanding, will guard [shield] your hearts and your minds in Christ Jesus.

4. In succession, work at each "knot" before the Lord, turning it this way and that, praying, "Lord, help. Lord, give me wisdom and solutions from You. I trust You. And by faith I examine this ugly knot *with thanksgiving."*

When you don't see a solution, let it go and turn to an easier knot. There are small ones God will help you free on the spot; tougher ones may depend on solving the smaller ones first.

5. Now deliberately, in spite of your tangle, turn your full attention to Jesus; focus your eyes on Him.

Sing to Him; perhaps you could sing a praise song. If all you know is "Jesus Loves Me," that's a great one. (Remember what music did for King Saul in 1 Samuel 16:23.)

As it says in Psalm 68:3-4,

> May the righteous be glad
> and rejoice before God;
> may they be happy and joyful.
> Sing to God, sing praise to his name.

(Remember, "the righteous" aren't perfect people—in our eyes—they're the ones who have received Jesus as their Savior and so *God sees* them as righteous, or perfect! Wonderful! And He says His plan, His will, is for them to be happy and joyful.)

Whether you feel like it or not, make a program every day of these three:

1. In a spirit of relaxation, gently working those "knots" one at a time,

2. Bible reading,

3. praise and singing—"let the afflicted . . . rejoice" (Psalm 34:2).

Did you know that personal joy is your strong defense against the world, the flesh, and the devil?

That truth is affirmed in two letters we received. One says,

> Our country is at war and our dear son is of prime drafting age, but we have peace in our hearts. Are we submitting to this? More than that, when God is in control we are actually *praising* Him for it.

The second letter is from a wife whose dearly loved husband has been found to have terminal cancer. She writes,

> God has given us the grace to face this, to speak and share it, and to believe that He is doing what is best. The last thing before surgery that Bill said to me was, "Remember, no matter which way it goes it will be RIGHT!"

Of course behind the scenes there are tears, there is pain. Moses went through every kind of turmoil, but "he persevered because he saw him who was invisible" (Hebrews 11:27).

Are your eyes focused upon Jesus and His solutions?

Maybe you're saying, "Anne, I just have too many knots. There's no hope; my life's a mess."

Let God speak to you, dear friend, through His mouthpiece Habakkuk. This prophet was facing international disasters on an overwhelming scale, and here's what he said:

Though the fig tree does not bud,
    and there are no grapes on the vines,
though the olive crop fails
    and the fields produce no food,
though there are no sheep in the pen and
    no cattle in the stalls. . .

[in other words, when everything all at once is absolutely terrible]

. . . yet I will rejoice in the Lord,
    I will be joyful in God my Savior.
The Sovereign LORD is my strength;
    he makes my feet like the feet of a deer,
    he enables me to go on the heights.

(Habakkuk 3:17-19)

God wants you "on the heights"—to live above it all—in Him, with Him. It's there, above the clouds, that the sun is always shining.

Let's pray together . . .

Thank You, Lord God, for alerting me to this danger. "Restore to me the joy of my salvation" (Psalm 51:12).

I don't see solutions yet, but I see that my sadness is the first part of the problem.

Lord, help me relax. Help me right now to turn my eyes upon Jesus.

And then, Lord, discipline me—to begin this daily program before You to overcome my sadness.

"I rejoice in following your statutes as one rejoices in great riches" (Psalm 119:14).

In Christ's name of power and authority, amen.

A parting
Glance

Then a new set of eyes
(so to speak) will develop within us,
enabling us to be looking at Jesus
while our outward eyes are seeing
the scenes of this passing world. . . .

—A.W. TOZER

SIX

When You're Angry

I have a memory of anger which is so childish I should have forgotten it—but I haven't. I can't.

I was a little girl, and my mother and I were having a tea party with my doll dishes. She was a great mom! But she said something that made me so frustrated I hit her arm, and the tea spilled all over everything. Some timing—I ruined the whole party. I still feel bad when I think of it.

No matter what a person's age, "a fool gives full vent to his anger" (Proverbs 29:11).

If you are angry at someone right now, you know the feeling in the pit of your stomach, and you know the words that race through your mind—words to tell that person and then words to tell others so they'll get on your side. . . .

Wait! Cool down. Be quiet a minute. Think.

Look at Jesus. He "endured" (Hebrews 12:2). He had every reason to be legitimately angry: Foolish, terrible people had unjustly done Him in. And yet He said, "Father, forgive them, for they do not know what they are doing" (Luke 23:34).

How can we defuse our anger, and the bitterness that comes with it? We need some kind of spiritual disciplines that will help to change our mental habit pattern. Perhaps the following little visual aid will do.

Get two sets of small pieces of paper—one set for mornings and one for your evenings.

On some of the papers write this:

> His compassions never fail.
> They are new every morning.
>
> (Lamentations 3:22-23)

Post these where you'll see them as you start each day: on the bathroom mirror, by the coffee pot, on your closet door. When you see them, commit your heart to feel compassion all that day for the person at whom you've been angry.

On the other pieces of paper write this:

> Do not let the sun go down
> while you are still angry.
>
> (Ephesians 4:26)

Post them where you'll see them as your day starts to wind down: on your car dashboard as you drive home from work, in your kitchen as you fix the evening meal, or at a desk where you do your home-work or go through your mail.

Then on another sheet of paper, check off each morning and each sundown that God has helped you to be compassionate and overcome your anger. And continue this for however long it takes to *melt that anger out of your heart and make you forgiving and compassionate and tender.*

You see, the problem isn't really the person who's troubling you; it's within you. All your life, sinners around you will sin—it's what they do best! But you don't have to let their behavior control your feelings.

Fix your eyes on Jesus. Remember His words:

> Love is patient, love is kind. . . . It is not
> easily angered, it keeps no record of
> wrongs. . . . It always protects, always
> trusts, always hopes, always perseveres.
> Love never fails (1 Corinthians 13:4-8).

If anger is your problem, you may suddenly realize that *Jesus' eye is fixed on you,* studying you, and He is asking you, "Doest thou well to be angry?" (Jonah 4:9 KJV). In other words, "Is this improving you?"

Anger tears down. It doesn't build up. Man's anger does not bring about the righteous life that God desires (James 1:20).

Would you like to melt the anger out of your heart?

Let's pray together . . .

Lord, I refuse to fix my eyes on those who trouble me, for then I get upset and feel abused and cheated and angry. Rather, I want to keep my eyes on You. Then my heart will melt, and I'll become like You—kind, compassionate, loving, forgiving. Help me, Lord!

In Your own dear name, amen.

Don't forget to post those pieces of paper!

Equipment can break down or get lost,
    water can leak away,
        records can be destroyed by fire,
    the minister can be delayed
        or the church burn down.
All these are external and subject to
            accident
    or mechanical failure. . . .
But looking is of the heart,
    and can be done successfully by
            anybody—
        standing up
        or kneeling down
        or lying in [your] last agony,
            a thousand miles from any church.

— A.W. TOZER,
THE PURSUIT OF GOD[3]

When You're Tempted

Temptation. A new one comes every day of the week.

Tomorrow is Sunday morning, and I'm here in the house all alone for the weekend—for long, precious hours to work on this book. The deadline is near.

Ray is at the National Religious Broadcasters' convention in Washington. He won't know if I go to church or not.

Melinda, our secretary, would normally be there, but she and John are out of town for the weekend. She wouldn't know.

The children are all involved in ministries in their own churches. They wouldn't know.

The church has two morning services; each of my friends would think I'd gone to the other one.

And here's the real cruncher: I just got the worst haircut of my entire life.

Lord, just this once, couldn't I stay holed up at home and keep writing about everybody's fixing their eyes on You?

Temptation!

Words from my own book *Up with Worship* came back to haunt me:

> Worship is fundamentally an offering. . . .
>
> Back in Old Testament days it was clear to see that worship involved giving. You came to the tabernacle or temple with your offering in your hand, or in your arms!—lugging it, or dragging it, maybe. It might have been wheat or oil, but often it was a sheep or goat or young bull. . . .
>
> And this is what worship still means today. Hebrew 13:15 says, "Through Jesus, therefore, let us continually offer to God a sacrifice of praise. . . ."
>
> The praise is to be continuous—which sometimes means inconvenient. It will take effort. . . .
>
> Sometimes you may be critically busy—when every minute of the day is precious, to get something done. Well, drag that lamb of two hours' time, and come to God's house.
>
> . . . Bring to Him your consistent, sacrificial gift of worship.
>
> Drag that lamb![4]

I hate it when my own words order me around. (Once Ray was driving on the freeway, feeling depressed. He turned on the radio and his own voice said, "Cheer up!" Ray scoffed, "Yeah, yeah, but what do *you* know about it?")

I'm going to church, of course. Would a cover-everything hat help? Well, I mustn't fix my eyes on myself. . . .

Late Sunday morning. Between my last words and now, I was hit with another, far more insidious temptation.

Last night I got into bed putting together in my head a story for this book which was almost true, but ever-so-slightly embellished—I could see in my mind's eye it would look just right on paper.

And there on television was an exposé of an itinerant preacher/healer who for years had "preached the Word" and cried "Praise Jesus" with the best of them. He had done it all. But now he was finally confessing that he had never even had a leaning toward the Christian religion! So after years of fraud, he was finally getting out of "the business."

Saddened and shocked, I vowed to straighten out my story, and I recommitted myself to honesty before the Lord in every part of me.

This morning, the choir sang "Panis Angelicus":

> And in temptation's hour,
>> Save through Thy mighty power. . . .

And during the quiet of the prelude, my eyes had fallen on Psalm 119:29-30:

> Keep me from deceitful ways . . .
> I have chosen the way of truth.

The sacrificial animals of Leviticus 1:9 *were washed in their inner parts,* to be "pleasing to the Lord."

> How much more, then, will the blood of
> Christ . . . cleanse our consciences . . . so
> that we may serve the living God!
> (Hebrews 9:14).

Are you tempted right now?

Is your mind coaxing you to yield?

Are your emotions strongly pulling you to yield?

Is your body screaming at you to yield?

Quick—force those eyes of yours to look to Jesus! He was tempted, too, you know.

And notice three things:

1. *God didn't cause Jesus' temptations, but He did allow them.* "Jesus was led by the Spirit into the desert to be tempted by the devil" (Matthew 4:1).

2. *Jesus' temptations were truly painful.* "He suffered when he was tempted" (Hebrews 2:18).

3. *Yet Jesus never once yielded.* "We have [a High Priest] who has been tempted in every way, just as we are—yet was without sin" (Hebrews 4:15).

Now let's look at those same three things in relation to your own temptation:

1. *God doesn't cause them, but He does allow them.* "When tempted, no one should say, 'God is tempting me.' . . . Each one is tempted when, by his own evil desire, he is dragged away and enticed" (James 1:13-14).

Be careful about that old saying, "You can't keep the birds from landing on your head—just don't let them build a nest in your hair." We use it to say, "It's no big deal if I'm tempted. Jesus was tempted, too."

Listen, you're not Jesus! Flap your arms! When they see your head or mine, they're positively *tempted* to land on us! These proverbial buzzards see inside of us our "evil desire," as James says, and they chirp, "Come on, everybody, that sucker's an easy touch. We can settle in there for sure." Then, as James goes on to say, the evil desire leads to sin, and the sin leads to death!

And it all begins with what we thought was a harmless little temptation.

2. *Your temptations, like Jesus', are truly painful.*

Run from them! Avoid them! Don't hang out where they might be! Jesus says, "Watch and pray so that you will not fall into temptation" (Matthew 26:41).

Over 400 years ago Francis de Sales wrote,

> As soon as you perceive yourself
> tempted, follow the example of children
> when they see a wolf or a bear in the
> country, for they immediately run into the
> arms of their father or mother. . . .
> Run in spirit to embrace the holy cross,
> as if you saw our Savior Jesus Christ cruci-
> fied before you. Protest that you never will
> consent to the temptation, implore His
> assistance against it, and still refuse your

consent as long as the temptation shall continue.

But . . . *look not the temptation in the face, but look only to our Lord* (emphasis added).[5]

Why? Because every time you fix your eyes on the temptation, you'll be that much weaker and more apt to yield.

"When the woman *saw* . . . the fruit of the tree . . . she *took* . . . it" (Genesis 3:6, emphasis added).

"Achan . . . *saw* . . . the plunder . . . and . . . *took*" (Joshua 7:20-21, emphasis added).

"David . . . *saw* a woman . . . and *took* her" (Samuel 11:2,4 KJV, emphasis added)

Watch, for instance, what you absorb of the daily news. Dirty people love dirt; that's why so much of the news is about dirt. So you, too, take it into your mind, you picture it, you imagine it. Now your own mind is dirty as well. And from a dirty mind springs dirty acts. The news media are powerful transmitters of moral diseases.

If you're struggling with a temptation so big that you're frightened, rush to a godly older person for counsel. Even the humiliation of confessing the temptation will strengthen you against it.

But it's not usually the big temptations that undo us, it's the lesser ones. It's not usually the wolves and bears that defeat us, it's the flies!

Which is harder for you to resist, murder or anger?

Adultery or those exciting but treacherous little flirtations?

Stealing or coveting?

Vile actions or vile thoughts?

Mafia connections or subtle craftiness and scheming?

Oh, the flies, the flies! Eventually they can make you feel as corrupted as if you were a chronic liar or a drunk.

This is all-out war. As long as you live, don't let down your guard.

But here's the good news:

3. *You don't have to yield.* "God is faithful; he will not let you be tempted beyond what you can bear. But when you are tempted, he will also provide a way out so that you can stand up under it" (1 Corinthians 10:13). And, "Because [Jesus] himself suffered when he was tempted, he is able to help those who are being tempted" (Hebrews 2:18).

So what do you do when you're tempted? You focus your eyes not on the temptation, but on Jesus. Then you'll "find grace to help . . . in [your] time of need" (Hebrews 4:16).

Dear Herman Wobbema! He knew that grace. Herman was a beautiful older man in our Lake Avenue Church, almost stone deaf, with a million-dollar smile.

Once in the middle of an evening service Ray suddenly held a microphone right to Herman's mouth; he was sitting in an aisle seat. Unforewarned, Herman said gently into the mike,

> Through many dangers, toils, and snares,
>   I have already come;
> 'Tis grace hath brought me safe thus far,
>   And grace will lead me home.

He never heard what followed: the whole congregation's spontaneous applause.

Let's pray together . . .

O Father, I'd like to cultivate Herman's perspective in my life! You know my dangers, my toils, my snares—but You promised they'll never be more than I can bear.

O Jesus, for courage and victory I call on Your grace. I fix my eyes on You. Amen.

When You're Misunderstood or Mistreated

The pain that comes when suffering at the hands of others can be great—especially when it's inflicted unjustly, or without reason. Is there anything harder to bear than undeserved suffering? If you're experiencing such pain now or have done so in the past, then fix your eyes on Jesus. I'm sure that sounds like a cliché but it's not, by any means. What does Jesus have to say to you?

The Lord Jesus knew that suffering is part of God's perfect and loving will. Ouch, that doesn't sound like good news! Keep reading; it's going to be.

> This suffering is all part of the work God has given you. Christ, who suffered for you, is your example (1 Peter 2:21 TLB).

Christians who don't believe their suffering is "of the Lord" turn out weak and unstable. At any encounters with pain they're apt to cry for immediate deliverance, thinking it's of the devil, or else they turn and run—from a job, a church, a marriage, whatever the cause of the pain.

Maybe they've never noticed Philippians 1:29:

> To you has been given the privilege not
> only of trusting him but also of suffering
> for him (TLB).

Trusting and suffering: the two come as a package. You take one, you get the other with it.

You take salvation from a good Father, you get the privilege of suffering from the same good Father.

You say "thank you" for one, you say "thank you" for the other (1 Thessalonians 5:18).

Understanding this simple truth makes strong, sturdy, unflappable believers. Through the worst circumstances their heads are up. Said Job, "Shall we accept good from God, and not trouble?"

Consider this: Your suffering isn't—or wasn't—really given to you by bad or thoughtless people.

No, it's God Himself, your wonderful Father, who— through people or circumstances—*permits suffering into your life. He lovingly allows it.*

> The testing of your faith develops perseverance. Perseverance must finish its work
> so that you may be mature and complete,
> not lacking anything (James 1:3-4).

He's shaping you by those pressures so you will turn out wonderful. He's perfecting you.

> He knows the way that [you] take; when he has tested [you, you will] come forth as gold (Job 23:10).

I'm counting on that. Ray and I spent some miserable years in a church where we didn't fit. It wasn't their fault! They were wonderful people and we still love them dearly; but we were just going different directions. The pain was terrible. But how valuable that suffering was for us! Ministering as we constantly do to pastors and their spouses, we would have been too glib, too self-assured, too full of easy answers, too unsympathetic—without that crashing failure in our own career.

And you, too, like the Lord Jesus Himself, are being "made perfect through suffering" (Hebrews 2:10). Isaiah 53:7,10 tells us that "He was oppressed and afflicted . . . Yet it was the LORD's will to crush him and cause him to suffer."

So what should you do when you suffer? Let's find out by looking at what Jesus did:

1. *He endured the cross.* "For the joy set before him [he] endured the cross" (Hebrews 12:2). And if you, too, "hang in there," your personal glory will follow as well. Romans 8:18 says that "our present sufferings are not worth comparing with the glory that will be revealed in us."

It won't be long! Jesus didn't run; He "endured." You do the same.

2. *But He scorned its shame.* Think about this carefully. To scorn means "to belittle." Jesus didn't scorn the *cross*—to suffer on the cross for the sins of the world was a Big Deal to Him. And for you to be called by God to participate in His sufferings (1 Peter 4:13)—that's a Big Deal, too. Appreciate it.

But the *shame* of the cross He did scorn; He took that part of it lightly. He thought little of His own humiliation, His own feelings. He wasn't self-centered, self-pitying.

3. *Even in His suffering, He was still concerned for others.* When He hung on the cross, Jesus made sure someone would take care of His mother. He entrusted her to the care of the apostle John: "He said to his mother, 'Dear woman, here is your son,' and to the disciple, 'Here is your mother.'" (John 19:26-27).

4. *He had true compassion on those who hurt Him.* "Father, forgive them (Luke 23:34). No bitterness, no vengeful thoughts, no demanding of rights.

5. *"He entrusted himself to him who judges justly"* (1 Peter 2:23). He prayed, "Father into your hands I commit my spirit" (Luke 23:46).

If you feel totally misunderstood—or if you have in the past, if you suffer at the hands of others—or if in the past you did, your first need is prayer.

Lord, for my own maturing, to make me more like Christ, You've allowed me to participate in His sufferings. I'm awed. I'm honored to be in such company. That's a Big Deal.

But Lord, I choose to belittle my own feelings. They're not a big deal. Keep me from retaliation, real or imagined; keep me from filling my thoughts with self-pity and fresh self-woundings and all over-occupation with myself.

Lord, keep my heart and life concerned for others.

Lord, give me true compassion for my oppressors.

And, Lord, I entrust myself totally to You. Into Your good hands I commit my spirit. Amen.

You're released! You're free! Your heart has begun a deep process of healing! Hold your head high!

Turning your eyes upon Jesus has lifted you above all your oppression. God is using it as an instrument to perfect you, mature you, make you whole.

"Consider it pure joy," James said (1:2).

Now you can read Romans 12:14-21 with new clarity:

> Bless those who persecute you. . . . Do not repay anyone evil for evil. . . . Do not take revenge . . . but leave room for God's wrath, for it is written: "It is mine to avenge; I will repay," says the Lord. On the contrary: "If your enemy is hungry, feed him; if he is thirsty, give him something to drink. . . ." Do not be overcome by evil, but overcome evil with good.

Let's pray together . . .

O Lord Jesus, I, Anne Ortlund, take this for myself as well. Help me not to write one thing and act another. May writer pray for reader, and reader for writer, that when we are misunderstood or mistreated, we may fix our eyes on You. Amen.

When You Struggle Financially

Our family has lived for several months at a time here and there overseas. Before we went the first time, we thought that Americans are worldly and materialistic because they have so much.

Then we discovered that *Christians overseas can be worldly and materialistic even though they have little!* Their focus can be on what they *don't* have—talking constantly about their high taxes, their low wages, how wonderful America must be, their frustrations over lacking this and lacking that.

Then we began thinking about Christians we know, American or otherwise, who are wealthy but not worldly, material-rich but not materialistic. They're responsible or even lavish in their giving: *Their eyes are on Jesus.*

And we know "poor" Christians who are the same!

And we thought, *Being materialistic means being too aware of the material, whether you have too much or little.*

For years Ray and I knew a famous California orange rancher—he's in heaven now—who gave to the Lord of his time and money beyond all human reasoning. Elbow-deep in ministry, he had little time to oversee his ranches. Privately one time he said to me as he shook his head in wonder, "Anne, it seems as if the more I stay away from those oranges, the more the Lord makes them multiply!" This man's eyes were truly fixed on Jesus.

Then Ray and I have a dear friend who spent most of her adult life as a nanny in a wealthy home, and when she reached retirement age ten years ago, they turned her out without a cent. I know very few of the miracle-stories about how God pays her apartment rent and keeps her from month to month, although I know her well. She's always too busy talking about other things: the schoolchildren's choir she helps with, the balloons she's blown up for somebody's birthday party, the fun she's having caring for some shut-in. . . . Her eyes are continually on Jesus, and He Himself provides for her.

Does this all sound too glib?

Do I sound insensitive to your struggles?

God has given Ray and me struggles, too. He gave us early-marriage poverty, with three babies and simply not enough food money to last between those small paychecks. He gave us later poverty, when at the age that most people retire we got stripped of our life savings. And along the way He gave us sudden joblessness, not of our choosing.

Then there's Jesus. He lived His earthly life in both poverty and serenity. He had almost nothing, and yet—for instance—He was confident that His Father would provide an upper room for the Last Supper.

Our friend Jim says, "Boy, it was so freeing when I discovered that my income isn't my source of supply, God is! God knows my needs, not my income! So I don't depend on my income; I depend on Him."

Read these words from the psalmist:

> The eyes of all look to you,
>   and you give them their food at the
>   proper time.
> You open your hand
> and satisfy the desires of every living
>   thing (Psalm 145:15-16).

To be dependent on your own supplies is bondage. To be dependent on Him (the One who promises over and over to supply your need)—that is freedom.

But let me ask you a question: Is your cash shortage temporary or chronic?

If it's temporary, wait upon Him for supply.

If you're chronically cash-short, something is wrong, because that doesn't fit with all His promises. Think about them:

The Lord is my shepherd,
   I shall not be in want (Psalm 23:1).

He provides food for those who fear him;
   he remembers his covenant forever
      (Psalm 111:5).

The Lord does not let the righteous go
   hungry (Proverbs 10:3).

What, then, is the problem? Is there a need for more discipline? Planning the budget? I encourage you to go to a financial advisor—best of all, a godly older couple or person who seems to have been wise in handling money.

Maybe you're overspending; you want too much too soon. The Lord says that's sin (Luke 15:13-18). Ask for help to set up a budget, and ask your advisor to hold you accountable to stick to it.

Maybe you're under-giving; the Lord says that's sin, too (Haggai 1:5-9). At the top of your budget items put your tithe, and make that the first check you write with every incoming paycheck.

Correct what you see isn't right—and then trust Him, trust Him, trust Him!

You can't support yourself any more than you could create yourself. Leave to God the things that only God can do. Don't fix your eyes on your bills, your problems, your needs—He knows your needs. (Matthew 6:32).

Let's pray together...

Abba Father, Your Word is so full of Your wonderful promises to care for me. Help me to relax in my heart and live by faith and not by sight.

O Lord, give me wisdom for earning, spending, saving, and giving. And help me to look to You for supply.

I thank You for seasons of plenty, and I thank You for seasons of want (Philippians 4:12-13). I know both are from Your loving hand, according to my deepest need.

I trust You! In Christ's strong name, amen.

All things are yours;
All are yours,
and you are of Christ,
and Christ is of God

(1 CORINTHIANS 3:21-23).

When you see that Christ is everything,
and you make Him your everything,
then you have everything.

PART THREE

Looking to Jesus to Shape Your Life

❧

Once it was the blessing,
  Now it is the Lord;
Once it was the feeling,
  Now it is His Word;
Once His gifts I wanted,
  Now the Giver own;
Once I sought for healing,
  Now Himself alone.

— A. B. Simpson

TEN

Shaping Your Goals

I have the ugliest, most comfy, most loved pair of old sweats. And I have the ugliest, most comfy, most loved pair of old Nikes. I tell Melinda, our secretary, I'm gonna wear my sweats and Nikes in heaven for-ever—unless I'm not supposed to wear anything at all. In which case, by then I'll look terrific.

Normally I only wear those uglies when I run, which is in our own neighborhood and pretty private. But the other day I had them on when I ducked briefly into the office, and Melinda and Ray both hooted when they saw my backside. I had a big split in the seam where I sit down.

This called for drastic action. I absolutely hate to sew, but that night I sat down with needle and thread and laboriously put my dear old sweats back together again.

Which is to say, no matter the awkwardness or pain or inconvenience, *most of us manage to do what we most want to do.*

What do you most want to do in your life? Whether you're following a carefully written list of personal goals or playing it by ear, you're probably doing it.

What is it you somehow manage to make room for, no matter what else must be sacrificed?

> Feeling good?
> Reading?
> Television?
> Weekends away in the R.V.?
> Your wardrobe?
> Your house?
> Certain relationships?
> Your job or career?
> Bowling?
> Skiing?
> Keeping up on the news?

Don't excuse, don't deceive yourself. Scrutinize your life to see if you have loves unworthy of eternity that are sacrosanct, inviolable. If you do, they're the "weights" of Hebrews 12:1. In themselves they're not sin but they will certainly hinder you.

And they degrade you. They make sure you don't get to be that great man or woman of God that you could otherwise become.

What a waste.

What a tragedy.

Read with me the final paragraph of Ray's little book, *Lord, Make My Life a Miracle:*

> Your danger and mine is not that we
> become criminals, but rather that we
> become respectable, decent, commonplace,
> mediocre Christians. The twentieth-cen-
> tury temptations that really sap our spiri-
> tual power are the television, banana
> cream pie, the easy chair, and the credit
> card. *The Christian wins or loses in those
> seemingly innocent little moments of* decision.
>
> Lord, make my life a miracle![6]

Are you ready for that moment in eternity when you will stand before Him and give an account?

> We must all appear before the judgment
> seat of Christ, that each one may receive
> what is due him for the things done
> while in the body, whether good or bad
> (2 Corinthians 5:10).

Verse 9 of that same passage answers how you can be ready:

> So we make it our goal to please him.

Above all else—*your goal is to please Him!* You scratch and claw for this; for this you discipline your-self; you get others to hold you accountable.

Come hell or high water, *you stretch to be, to do, what pleases Him.* Whatever it costs you, it's worth it. It's the fine pearl for which you sell everything so you can buy it (Matthew 13:45-46).

To please Him, you sacrifice, if need be,

> feeling good,
> reading,
> television,
> weekends away in the R.V.,
> your wardrobe,
> your house,
> certain relationships,
> your job or career,
> your bowling,
> your skiing,
> your keeping up on the news,
> and anything else that weighs you down.

Is that your life goal? To please Him?

You can break down that goal into more specific yearly goals, maybe three-month goals, today's goals. Make them practical; make them measurable.

And remember, pleasing Him will work out differently in your life than in anyone else's because He has made you unique.

> [You] are God's workmanship, created in
> Christ Jesus to do good works, which God
> prepared in advance for [only you] to do
> (Ephesians 2:10).

Be very careful, then, how you live . . .
understand what the Lord's will is (Ephesians 5:15,17).

And get tough, says 1 Corinthians 9. Don't
pamper your body; beat it and make it your slave:

Do you not know that in a race all the runners
run, but only one gets the prize? Run in such a way as
to get the prize. Everyone who competes in the games
goes into strict training (1 Corinthians 9:24-25).

Let's pray together . . .

*O Lord, I deliberately refuse to gaze fondly at my toys,
my conveniences, my pleasures, my comfort zones. I want
to fix my eyes on You. I want to make it my life goal, and
my day-by-day goal, to please You.*

> *As the eyes of slaves look to the hand of
>   their master,*
> *As the eyes of a maid look to the hand of
>   her mistress,*
> *So [my] eyes look to [You] (Psalm 123:2).*

*Show me Your will, O Lord, and help me to do it.
That's what You most want, and now that's what I most
want—so it will please us both. For Your own sake, amen.*

I thank Thee for showing me the vast
    difference
  between knowing things by reason
  and knowing them by the spirit
    of faith.
By reason I see a thing is so;
  by faith I know it as it is.
I have seen Thee by reason and have
    not been amazed,
I have seen Thee as Thou art in
    the Son
  and have been ravished to behold
    Thee.

— OLD PURITAN PRAYER

ELEVEN

Shaping Continual Fellowship with Him

The first night I was a pastor's wife I didn't get much of a chance to sleep.

Ray and the three babies and I had moved from Princeton Seminary in New Jersey to our first pastorate in Christiana, Pennsylvania, a town with 1,100 souls, counting absolutely everybody.

You know how moving is.

The children were finally bedded down, Buddy and Margie in their cribs and Sherry on a mattress on the floor. Then the doorbell rang, and a sad-looking lady stood there. Her mother was dying, and she didn't want to care for her alone. Would I come help?

I went to Mrs. Thompson's house. We slept in snatches, but much of the time it seemed we were trying to pry Mother's teeth apart to get down pills with teaspoons of water. In the morning I went home again to our new house, a little shaky in the legs.

Was this how it was to be a pastor's wife? Would people call on me every night to help the dying? (Mrs. Thompson's mother died later that morning, and nobody has ever asked me to do that since.)

But there was a special wonder to that first full day in the ministry. I was groggy, but I asked the Lord for His presence to be my strength, and I lived it in living color. *Life was precious. Death was a reality. Somebody had truly needed me and been truly helped.*

The presence of the Lord was all around me, cheering me, reassuring me. I was so aware of His hand on me, His guidance, His mercy.

Perhaps He made it rough on me that first 24 hours so that I would early on begin to *keep my eyes on Him* and discover His nearness, His availability.

Maybe you're saying, "Be practical, Anne. How do I get this habit of being continually aware of Him?"

I'm still learning myself, but I do have two suggestions.

First, ask Him. I know what I do when left to myself: I'm "prone to wander—Lord, I feel it!—prone to leave the God I love." *Ask Him.* He loves you to.

Second, cooperate with Him. Vote against your natural waywardness! Keep prompting yourself, to form the habit.

Ray writes "PTP" (Practice the Presence) on those little post-it papers and plasters them on his dashboard, desk, mirror.

If he feels he's really forgetting too much, he sets his wristwatch alarm to go off every fifteen minutes.

I know a housewife who's conditioned herself to remember the Lord whenever she walks through her kitchen door.

I know a working gal who hears Westminster chimes every fifteen minutes from a nearby city clock, and she sings with it her own words: 'I love You, Lord; Lord, You are here....'

When you're conscious of Him, what do you do?

Talk. "Pray continually," says 1 Thessalonians 5:17.

> "Help me in what I'm doing right now...."
> "I love You, Lord...."
> "Forgive me...."
> "Bless the person I'm talking to...."

Catch the flavor of Nehemiah's inner habit:

> The king said to me, "What is it you want?" Then I prayed to the God of heaven, and I answered the king...
> (Nehemiah 2:4-5).

Or again,

> All Judah brought the tithes of grain, new wine and oil into the storerooms. I put [certain men] in charge....Remember me for this, O my God (Nehemiah 13:12-14).

You'll enjoy the happiest, most comfortable life possible when you keep a running conversation going with Him. He loves it, and you'll love it.

Think of a sponge plunged into the ocean. It soaks up the sea until it's totally saturated. Yet—it's still a sponge.

Think of yourself fixing your eyes on Jesus. You're plunged into an awareness of His presence, surrounding you wherever you go. You "soak up" the Lord and all His characteristics until you're saturated. And yet you're still you.

But this habit doesn't just "happen." *It begins with desire, and it continues with discipline.* It's not just automatic, it's learned—like somebody's being initiated into a fraternity or sorority, until they're at last in the fellowship:

> Blessed are those who have learned to
>   acclaim you,
>   who walk in the light of your presence,
>   O LORD.
> They rejoice in your name all the day long;
>   they exult in your righteousness.
> For you are their glory and strength
>   (Psalm 89:15-17).

The ocean becomes the sponge's very own wateriness and saltiness.

The Lord becomes your very own glory and strength. You receive all your achievements, your happiness, your well-being from what is continually surrounding you: the presence God Himself.

Start soaking Him in right now. And check in ten minutes from now, and ten minutes after that. . . .*The presence of God in your life will become your glory and your strength.*

Moses insisted on it (Exodus 33:15).

David wouldn't live without it (Psalm 27:8).

If you don't have this glory and this strength, my friend, then you're pretty much like any other wife or bank teller or mother or corporation employee or whatever. It's either the presence of God in your life—

> purifying
> empowering
> continual

—or else it's just you alone trying to do the best you can. And that just doesn't make it.

Does the thought of practicing His presence seem burdensome to you? Do a bird's wings weigh it down?

Do yourself a favor.

Do your emotions a favor.

Do your physical body a favor.

Keep your eyes fixed continually on Jesus.

Let's pray together . . .

Lord, as I keep reading this book, may I be most conscious neither of Anne Ortlund nor of myself; may I be most conscious of You. Keep me looking at You, Lord. Teach me—by means of these words or in spite of these words; may the teaching come primarily from You.

I Want to See You, Lord

Throughout the reading of the book, Lord, and then afterwards when I move on to other things, may I be a sponge in sea water, soaking You up! Help me to maintain the habit, both now and in the future. Keep my eyes fixed on You! In Your name, amen.

Never separate yourself from God.
  How sweet it is
to live always near those who love us!

— Gold Dust

Shaping a Daily "Quiet Time"

Cartoon seen recently:

A fellow is listening uncertainly as a recorded voice says out of his telephone receiver, "Your number cannot be completed as dialed. Please check the number you are calling and dial again. Or ask yourself if talking to another person is what you really need at this moment!"

Sometimes your need is just to be quiet.

At least once a day, you need to back off from all the other voices and hear only His. It needs to be a long enough time to be meaningful—to express your love, confess your sins, receive guidance, delight in Him, *listen.*

I have an electric toothbrush that needs frequent plugging into the socket to get re-juiced. And you and I can't go anywhere for very long without the sacrifice of times of quiet with God to get restored again.

Notice that I said *sacrifice*.

A thirty-ish woman said to me at a conference two days ago, "There's no way I can have a daily quiet time. I have five small children who take everything I've got, and then I work every day from four to midnight." As I questioned her, I discovered she has a working husband and almost no debts.

She stood there, weepy, overweight, defeated. It would mean true sacrifice for her to add time with the Lord to her exhausting days. But *until she does, she may not hear His solutions and so she'll spiral ever farther downward.*

Whatever your circumstances—if you'd lived in Old Testament times you would have regularly given God a male animal or bird—whatever you could afford—that had no defects: something you'd humanly want or even "need" for yourself.

What can you give to God today?

If you're stressed out from a tight schedule, offer God the sacrifice of your time.

If you love to be with people, give Him the sacrifice of your solitude.

If you're not very excited yet about Bible reading and prayer, lift up to Him the sacrifice of your surrendered will.

And when you sit down or kneel to be with Him, what do you do?

No two people will have quiet times just alike, but first decide on a time, a place, and a plan—and stick to it.

Since the time my children started school, I've chosen mid-mornings—my high-energy time. I have with me my Bible, my notebook, and a pen.

First, in the prayer section of my notebook, I put the date and I write that day's prayers to Him. Maybe I should read my Bible first for a while? Some people prefer to do that. Anyway, my current habit is to pray first.

I write out my prayers to God in complete sentences, as if I were writing to a friend. Sometimes I structure sections of my prayer to the acronym ACTS: *adoration, confession, thanksgiving,* and *supplication.* That keeps me from getting the "gimmies" too much.[7]

In any case, writing my prayers has probably been the greatest single encouragement I've ever had in my walk with the Lord! Practically, it keeps my mind from wandering, and it monitors how much time each day I'm actually giving Him in undistracted prayer—so I can't fool myself.

The Big Bonus has been discovering how seriously God takes my requests! Weeks or months later I've looked back and read over earlier prayers, and been amazed to see how He's started the wheels of heaven turning to bring about the things I asked of Him!

Then I take up His Word, still with notebook and pen in hand.[8]

For years Ray and I have read straight through the Bible annually. Of course, any way you read through God's Word will bring blessing—but this is what I said to my eager young friend Cathy the other day. I urged her not to dip from Old Testament to New Testament to Psalms and back again. I said that's like trying to explore a mountain by being blindfolded and helicoptered into one section and studying that; then being blindfolded again and helicoptered into another section and studying that.

The Bible is a *book*. It goes from start to finish, unfolding stories and developing themes as it goes. Get the sweep of the whole, over and over! Five pages a day will do it in a year.

Oh, how I love my personal Bible! Each year in the margins I write comments and cross-references and brief prayers concerning what I'm reading, along with the date beside it. Then each year I come to those roadmarks again. My Bible represents my personal walk with God for a period of three or four years, and when it's filled and ragged, I start over with another Bible. Right now I'm finishing up the fourth year with this beloved, tattered old Bible, and because the Exodus 13–14 page is detached, the Israelites are having trouble getting across the Red Sea.

They keep wandering off onto my lap.

Let's pray together...

Lord, I need more prayer and more of Your Word in my life! Show me how to schedule these and how to structure them, to be diligent, consistent, making progress. Guide me to the right helps.

My problem is desire, Lord! Stir me up, O Holy Spirit of God. Help me to thirst for, to crave the Word (1 Peter 2:2). It's what I need, what those around me need, what the world needs. And as I flood it with prayer, it will help me grow in grace as well as in knowledge (2 Peter 3:18).

Lord, I consecrate myself to You for this. In myself I will fail; that's why I want to keep my eyes on You.

In Christ's lovely name, amen.

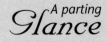
A parting
Glance

*Prayer ... indicates to God that
someone would speak to Him,
and God, so good and gracious,
is ever ready to listen (with all
reverence we say it) with the prompt
attention of a faithful servant.*

— GOLD DUST

THIRTEEN

Shaping Your Service to Him

Why do you do voluntary service?

> Because you enjoy it?
> Because it makes you a better person?
> Because it pleases your pastor or your spouse or someone else?
> Because you feel you need to pitch in and do your share?

There were "church workers" called Levites in Ezekiel 44 whom God *exposed* as serving for the reasons above!

They had their eyes on themselves and on others, but not on Him.

This particular group of Levites had had a long history of serving themselves and other people—to the point of even helping others in their idol worship! (Correct doctrine isn't too important to you when you get carried away wanting to please other people.)

And God said, "All right, from now on just please people, not Me. You weren't focused on Me before; from now on I won't *allow* you to be. You can keep on doing church 'busy work,' but I won't let you minister to Me Myself."

It makes all the difference.

An eye fixed on self is full of confusion: "How much commitment is commitment? If I teach a Sunday school class can I never go away on weekends? If I join the choir, what happens when choir practice night comes and I'm exhausted?"

The "me generation" says, "I can only be somewhat committed to you because I'm first committed to me."

> [A man] said, "I will follow but first let me
> go back and say good-by to my family."
> Jesus replied, "No one who puts his hand
> to the plow and looks back is fit for
> service in the kingdom of God" (Luke
> 9:61-62).

But fix your eyes on Jesus, and you yourself will be helped the most.

An eye fixed on service to others is full of politics, and the service is performed in

> bossiness
> fussiness

competition
criticalness
self-will
ego

But fix your eyes on Jesus, and others will be helped the most.

You have access to the Lord Himself! Don't stop short in the vestibule.

Are you a ministry-centered person? You'll get depleted, irritated and abrasive, exhausted.

Are you a Christ-centered person? Even as you serve Him, you'll stay nourished, happy, rested.

Let's pray together . . .

Let's talk to Him about our service—I, Anne Ortlund, and you, too—through an old Puritan prayer:

> *O my Lord,*
>
> *Forgive me for serving Thee in sinful ways—*
>
> > *by glorying in my own strength,*
> > *by forcing myself to minister through necessity,*
> > *by accepting the applause of others,*
> > *by trusting in assumed grace and spiritual affection,*
> > *by a faith that rests on my hold on Christ, not on Him alone. . . .*

Help me to see
>> *that it is faith stirred by grace that does the*
>>>> *deed . . .*
>> *that faith centers in Thee as God all-*
>>>> *sufficient,*
>>> *Father, Son, Holy Spirit . . .*

If I have not such faith I am nothing. . . .
Keep me in a faith that works by love,
>> *and serves by grace. Amen.*

FOURTEEN

Shaping Your Perspective on Life

Parts of your life will be good, maybe even wonderful.

Parts of your life will be bad, maybe awful.

Don't fix your eyes too much on any of it. If you look too much at the good you'll become cocky. If you look too much at the bad you'll feel defeated. Anyway, what's good today may be bad tomorrow, and what's bad today may be wonderful tomorrow.

Nowhere does the Bible say to put your hope in life improvement; you'd spend your days in fear of disappointment.

Hope in God. Fix your eyes on Him, and let Him give you what He wants to, *for it will all turn out to be good.*

I get such a kick out of reading the old Christian classics. The truths don't change, but the terms do.

One seventeenth-century writer was commenting about people who came back to his area of Europe from visiting Peru.

He said they brought back gold and silver, but they were also apt to bring apes and parrots— "because they neither cost much, nor are burdensome"! (Can you believe it? I don't know, I think traveling with apes might be burdensome—maybe that means I'm a sissy.)

And so, he continues, when good things happen to you, accept them like parrots and apes—enjoy them—"provided they don't cost [you] too much care and attention, nor involve [you] in trouble, anxiety, disputes or contentions"!

(I can see the possibility of apes causing anxiety.)

His point is, don't let nice things in your life distract you from fixing your eyes on Jesus.

(This sage advice from long ago also suggests that if you *really* get elevated, try to accept what comes from your admirers "with prudence and discretion, accompanied by charity and suavity of manners"! Does that strike you as funny, too? Whatever good things come, don't forget to be suave!)

But through the centuries God's wise ones emphasize the same thing: "Fix your eyes. Fix your eyes."

William Law said around 1750 that everyone fixes his eyes on something; he interpreted that as "praying without ceasing." He said people pray continually as long as they're alive, because it's part of human nature.

> The [person] whose heart habitually tends
> toward the riches, honors, powers, or plea-
> sures of this life, is in a continual state of
> prayer toward all these things. His spirit
> stands always bent towards them. They
> have his hope, his love, his faith, and
> are . . . in reality the God of his heart.[9]

Can you see how, whenever we think something is lacking or in short supply in our life, we could easily "pray without ceasing" toward that?

> —in a jail cell, pray without ceasing
> toward release
> —in poverty, pray toward money
> —under an oppressive government,
> toward freedom
> —in loneliness, toward companionship

All the peoples of the world, each lacking *something,* can fix their eyes on their particular lack and be always restless, complaining, ungrateful, unhappy.

I'm speaking to myself as well: In your good times, in your bad times, when life is wonderful, when life is awful—don't fix your eyes on your life.

Instead, keep your eyes on Jesus.

This little gem was on my "Keswick calendar" recently:

> "Live while you live," the epicure would
> say,

"And seize the pleasures of the present
     day."
"Live while you live," the faithful
     preacher cries,
"And give to God each moment as it
     flies."
Lord, in my view, let each united be:
I live in pleasure while I live for Thee.[10]

I'm writing more than I've attained, but it both motivates and stabilizes me to read this other quotation from that same remarkable William Law, written also around 1750:

> The pious soul that eyes only God . . . can
> have no stop in its progress; light and
> darkness equally assist him. In the light he
> looks up to God. In the darkness he lays
> hold of God, and so they both do him the
> same good.[11]

Let's pray together . . .

O Father! I confess to You I don't yet have a deep conviction in my heart that darkness and light are equal. Lord Jesus Christ! I want to develop before You a "holy carelessness." I have a long way to go, but that phrase makes my mouth water.

Teach me to be without concern concerning all that concerns me—knowing that I am totally in Your perfect hands.

Teach me to fix my eyes on You, and to take what You give with poise and gratitude.

Teach me to say with Paul, "I have learned to be content whatever the circumstances. I know what it is to be in need, and I know what it is to have plenty. I have learned the secret of being content in any and every situation" (Philippians 4:11-12).

Teach me that secret, Lord Jesus. Amen.

Let us fix our eyes on Jesus . . .
>   *that He may cast us down, and that*
>   *He may raise us up;*
>   *that He may afflict us, and that He*
>   *may comfort us;*
>   *that He may despoil us, and that He*
>   *may enrich us;*
>   *that He may teach us to pray, and*
>   *that He may answer our prayers;*
>   *that while leaving us in the world,*
>   *He may separate us from it,*
>   *our life being hidden with*
>   *Him in God,*
>   *and our behavior bearing witness*
>   *to Him before men.*

—THEODORE MONOD,
EARLY TWENTIETH CENTURY

FIFTEEN

Shaping Your Perspective on Death

I was listening yesterday to the "Haven of Rest" radio broadcast. My favorite keyboardist, Duane Condon, was accompanying magnificently, and one of my favorite singers, bass Glenn Shoemaker, was singing "Guide Me, O Thou Great Jehovah."

(I listen to "Haven," on which Ray is the speaker, every morning at eight. I do things before and after, but at eight I turn on the little bathroom radio and dress and put on my face while I'm listening.)

Duane and Glenn came to verse three, and their music became slower, more majestic, and charged with triumphant exhilaration:

> When I tread the verge of Jordan,
> Bid my anxious fears subside;
> Death of death and hell's destruction

[What magnificent names for Christ!]
Land me safe on Canaan's side;
Songs of praises, songs of praises
I will ever give to Thee,
I will ever give to Thee.

I thought of my precious friend Becky, in my small group of disciples last year, who just the day before had died of cancer, barely 30 years old. I leaned into the mirror to put cover-up on some wrinkles. And though I love her and I miss her already, I thought, *You lucky rascal, Becky! You beat me there.*

I remember Ray preaching one time about Lazarus dying and his sisters' grief and Jesus raising Lazarus again. With tongue in cheek, Ray described the scene:

Lazarus is up in heaven. He's been there four days, and it's fantastic. He's gotten his robe and his golden shoes and they've already started him on his harp lessons.

Then he gets the news.

"Lazarus, you gotta go back."

"What? *Go back?* No way. Why?"

"The girls want you."

Lazarus groans. "The girls? You gotta be kidding . . . do I have to go?"

He finally gets persuaded, and he starts taking off his golden shoes. He hangs his robe and his harp in the locker he's been assigned, and he says, "Fellas, don't touch those things, my name's on them. And look, I'll be back!"

And he struggles back into his lousy old grave wrappings. . . .

If we had any idea how wonderful the next life is, we wouldn't hang onto this one so tenaciously!

Of course the pain of losing loved ones—though temporarily—is real enough. We don't "grieve like the rest of men, who have no hope" (1 Thessalonians 4:13), but we do grieve—sometimes terribly, deeply, excruciatingly in our loss.

But as far as death goes, we can be absolutely light-hearted. We've been freed from all fear of it (Hebrews 2:15); it has no more victory over us, no sting (1 Corinthians 15:55).

That wonderful Twenty-third Psalm says,

> Even though I walk through the valley of
> the shadow of death, I will fear no evil.

If a truck runs over you, you can get really ruined. But what happens when the *shadow* of a truck runs over you?

Psalm 23 speaks only of your walking through the *shadow* of death. Is that all?

In your thinking about dying, get Jesus' perspective.

And when your own time comes to die, focus your eyes on Him.

> Stephen, full of the Holy Spirit, looked up
> to heaven [the King James Version says
> "looked up steadfastly"] and saw the glory
> of God, and Jesus standing at the right
> hand of God. "Look," he said,

"I see heaven open...." Then ... he fell
asleep (Acts 7:55-56,60).

• • •

When the waters are rough and the sky is
dark, look towards the shore; the lights
shining there will attract and encourage
you. Stephen saw those lights....

There, where his Savior was, was his desti-
nation, his home, and from thence came
the grace and power that carried him
through.[12]

Are your eyes fixed on Jesus? Come, let's sing this
song to Him:

Precious Lord, take my hand, lead me on,
    help me stand;
  I am tired, I am weak, I am worn;
Through the storm, through the night,
    lead me on to the light;
  Take my hand, precious Lord, lead me home.
When my way grows drear, precious Lord,
    linger near,
  When my life is almost gone;
Hear my cry, hear my call, hold my hand lest I fall:
  Take my hand, precious Lord, lead me home.
When the darkness appears and the night
    draws near,
  And the day is past and gone,
At the river I stand, guide my foot, hold
    my hand,
  Take my hand, precious Lord, lead me
    home.[13]

PART FOUR

Looking to Jesus for Biblical Understanding

*L*ooking unto Jesus
(Hebrews 12:2).
Only three little words,
but in those three little words
is the whole secret of life.

—THEODORE MONOD
EARLY TWENTIETH CENTURY

SIXTEEN

Understanding Jesus, the Radiance of God's Glory

Everything you learn about Jesus Christ, as you look and look, is so magnificent that you could never adequately explain Him to anyone else.

A tribesman once "fixed his eyes" for the first time on the ocean. He was flabbergasted! He got a quart jar to take some back so he could show his people.

Jesus Christ is "the radiance of God's glory and the exact representation of his being" (Hebrews 1:3), "the exact likeness of the unseen God" (Colossians 1:15 TLB).

> No angel in the sky
> Can fully bear that sight,
> But downward bends his wond'ring eye
> At mysteries so bright.[14]

But though angels may look down, God commands you in Hebrews 12:2 to gaze studiously at Jesus, this One who is the very "radiance" of God's glory.

Fix your eyes on Him.

Look at what you're looking at.

When you look through a toy kaleidoscope and twist the tube, the bits of colored glass keep changing patterns over and over. Similarly, when you look at Jesus Christ to see God's glory, that glory will be "new every morning," always different, always beautiful.

"Show me your glory," Moses begged the Lord God.

No one may see me and live," said God. I will put you in a cleft in [a certain] rock and cover you with my hand until I have passed by. Then I will remove my hand and you will see my back" (Exodus 33:22-23). (His *back?* Moses had asked to see His *glory.* God is so mysterious.)

When God put Moses there in the rock, what was the glory of God that He allowed Moses to see?

He "saw" a proclamation of His name—that God is

> The LORD, the LORD,
> the compassionate and gracious God,
> slow to anger,
> abounding in love and faithfulness,
> maintaining love to thousands,
> and forgiving wickedness, rebellion
> and sin.
> Yet he does not leave the guilty unpunished (Exodus 34:6-7).

Look now through the kaleidoscope at Jesus Christ, "the radiance of God's glory" (Hebrews 1:3). Twist the tube a little.

God told Moses that He's the Lord. *See Christ transfigured on the mountain, His face shining. . . .* Twist the tube.

God told Moses He doesn't leave the guilty unpunished. *Look! Christ is whipping the moneychangers out of the Temple. . . .* Twist the tube.

God told Moses He maintains love to thousands. *See Christ feeding 5,000 hungry people. . . .*

Keep looking and looking at Christ, and you'll keep seeing new facets of the glory of God.

And yet all this, so far, is only His back! What will be the rest of God's glory, which will be revealed when you see His face?

Let's pray together . . .

O Lord Jesus, because You are all-important, all-worthy, I press on to keep my eyes on You! In Your incomparable name, amen.

SEVENTEEN

Understanding Jesus as Seen in the Bible

I remember ministering with Ray in Brazil and being in utter fatigue. In between meetings I'd lie on the bed and think, "I absolutely cannot get up again."

Then in my through-the-Bible daily reading I came to 2 Chronicles 15:7:

> But as for you, be strong and do not give
> up, for your work will be rewarded.

That day *God gave that verse just to me*—and I received it. And it was wonderful! I suddenly had all the pep I needed. In less than ten days we were ministering in Japan, and I was bouncing with energy.

And not that I couldn't—but so far I've never felt that deep fatigue again.

Later on during that same Brazil trip, while on a plane flying in the interior, I sat by a bright-faced young guy with a Bible. We spoke no common language, but I showed him on my page my wonderful new verse. He looked it up in his Portuguese Bible and glowed. Then he pointed out another page in his Bible, and I looked up that one:

> Stand firm. Let nothing move you. Always
> give yourselves fully to the work of the Lord,
> because you know that your labor in the
> Lord is not in vain (1 Corinthians 15:58).

And on we went, swapping marvelous verses and fellowshiping together. What a thrill! We parted with a hug.

There is no book like this book—for two reasons.

First, from cover to cover, it reveals Jesus Christ so you can look long and intimately at Him.

You know the New Testament is about Him; it was written after His life, death, and resurrection. But the Old Testament was written centuries before; is that about Him, too?

"Absolutely," said Jesus. "These are the scriptures that testify about me" (John 5:39).

Let's take a look.

In the Old Testament's very first book God promised Abraham,

> For all the land which thou seest, to thee
> will I give it, and to thy seed forever
> (Genesis 13:15 KJV).

And two thousand years later in the New Testament, the Spirit of God explains that He was talking in Genesis about Jesus Christ:

> He saith not, "And to seeds," as of many,
> but as one, "And to thy seed," which is
> Christ (Galatians 3:1 KJV).

Here's Psalm 110:1, written a thousand years before Jesus came to earth:

> The LORD says to my Lord: "Sit at my right
> hand until I make your enemies a footstool
> for your feet."

Jesus said this verse referred to Himself (Mark 12:35-37). It was Jehovah speaking to Adonai—the Father speaking to the Son.

And Peter, preaching on Pentecost in Acts 2, said the Psalms of David talked about Jesus of Nazareth.

Then there's Hebrews 1:8, which says Psalm 45:6-7 refers to Jesus.

And around 750 B.C. the prophet Isaiah wrote,

> I saw the Lord seated on a throne, high
> and exalted, and the train of his robe filled
> the temple (Isaiah 6:1).

What an awesome sight!

And John reveals whom Isaiah saw: the preexistent Christ—"Isaiah . . . saw Jesus' glory" (John 12:41).

It's been said of the Bible that "New is in the Old contained; The Old is by the New explained."

From Genesis to Revelation *Jesus is there,* and if you want to fix you eyes on Him, you must look at His entire book. A.W. Tozer used to say, "Nothing less than a whole Bible can make a whole Christian."[15]

Dr. Donald Grey Barnhouse was an American preacher of the last generation, and nobody ever sparkled when he preached like Dr. Barnhouse.

One time he was telling his audience why they needed to read the whole Bible. He reminded them how God said to Abraham, "I'm going to give you this land [Palestine], so go walk around it. Every place you set your foot will be yours" (his paraphrase of Genesis 13:14,17; Deuteronomy 11:24; and Joshua 1:3).

The way Dr. Barnhouse told it, that evening Abraham took a walk, walking around about an acre—and that night he owned an acre.

The next day he walked about a mile, and he owned the mile.

And when the sheep had grazed there, he took them over to the next valley, and he owned the valley. ("Every place where you set your foot will be yours.")

It wasn't too many years before he owned everything from Dan to Beersheba—just by putting his foot down.

And, said Dr. Barnhouse with his sparkle, many Christians possess a very small Bible. They have John 3:16 and the Twenty-third Psalm and a few other little passages, and they keep going back and forth from one to another, maybe grazing those little spots down to bare rock. And that's all they have.

But God says, "Go, walk through the length and breadth of the land! Every place where you set your foot will be yours"—full of wonderful truths just for you.

Take up your Bible; look at it. The land is before you, ready for you to possess.

And *Jesus is there!* "Handle me, and see," He says (Luke 24:39 KJV).

So read your Bible from cover to cover, for two reasons.[16]

First, as we already said, because it reveals Jesus Christ to you.

And *second, because it reveals yourself to you!*

"What?" you're asking. "What do you mean?"

Well, you have to agree, being humans, that we're definitely more curious to read a book about ourselves than about others. While it's true that the Bible is about Jesus, it's also about you.

I would think one reason Jesus loved the Old Testament, the Scriptures of His day, is just what we've been saying: because they were full of Him. In them He saw Himself. And wouldn't they have been a powerful motivation for Him to fulfill everything that He saw written about Himself?

When He felt depleted from healing people (Mark 5:30), what a thrill to remember what Isaiah had predicted:

Surely he took up our infirmities and carried our sorrows (Isaiah 53:4; see also
Matthew 8:17).

When He was physically exhausted from teaching
by parables—sometimes to thousands at once with no
microphone—how fulfilling it must have been to
remember that Asaph the musician had sung a psalm
that one day He would do just that:

> I will open my mouth in parables,
> I will utter hidden things, things from of
>   old (Psalm 78:2; see also Matthew
>   13:34-35).

And when He needed "go-power" to face that
excruciating cross, how He must have held before His
eyes the prophecy,

> He will not falter or be discouraged
> till he establishes justice on earth
>   (Isaiah 42:4)!

And here's the remarkable thing: the Bible not
only describes Jesus, *it also describes you.* His likeness
is there—but so is yours. God gives you in His Word
a picture of what He means for you to be:

> Completely humble and gentle . . . patient
>   (Ephesians 4:2)
> Strong in the Lord and in His mighty
>   power (Ephesians 6:10)
> Without complaining or arguing
>   (Philippians 2:14)

Not anxious, guarded by peace
(Philippians 4:6-7)
Forgiving, loving (Colossians 3:13-14)
Encouraging one another
(1 Thessalonians 5:11)
Respectful of leadership (1 Thess-
alonians 5:12)
Always joyful (1 Thessalonians 5:16)
Continually praying (1 Thess-
alonians 5:17)
Giving thanks in all circumstances
(1 Thessalonians 5:18)
Avoiding every kind of evil (1 Thess-
alonians 5:22)
Hard working (2 Thessalonians 3:11-13)
Watching for the Lord's return (1 Thess-
alonians 1:10)
More than conquerors (Romans 8:37)!

So *love the Scriptures,* as Jesus did. Search there for God's picture of your own intended image and likeness, and then seek to fulfill through your own life and personality exactly what you see.

When you fix your eyes on Jesus as seen in the Bible, you're fixing your eyes on aspects and characteristics of Him that God wants you to have as well.

Then you will "reflect the Lord's glory, [and be] transformed into his [own] likeness with ever-increasing glory, which comes from the Lord" (2 Corinthians 3:18)!

Let's pray together . . .

O Lord, what a vision You have set before me! Now give me a heart to pursue this vision, the discipline to fulfill it.

> Beyond the sacred page
>   I seek Thee, Lord. . . .
>
> Open my eyes that I may see wonderful
>   things in your law (Psalm 119:18).
>
> The commands of the LORD are radiant,
>   giving light to the eyes (Psalm 19:8).

Father, as I probe Your Word, help me to fix my eyes on Jesus, "the eyes of [my] heart may be enlightened, that [I] may know the hope to which he has called [me]" (Ephesians 1:18).

In His dear name, amen.

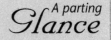

A parting Glance

[Fix your eyes on] Jesus in the Scriptures,
to learn there what He is,
what He has done,
what He gives,
what He desires;
to find in His character our pattern,
in His teachings our instruction,
in His precepts our law,
in His promises our support,
in His person and in His work
a full satisfaction provided for every
need of our souls.

—THEODORE MONOD

Understanding Jesus, the Son of Man

The come and go of busy feet
With sound of hammer down the busy street,
A little two-roomed house with scarce a breath
Of air; in busy, crowded Nazareth.
Yes, here for love of thee, through silent years—
Oh, pause and see, if thou art wise—
The King of kings dwelt in disguise.[17]

Jesus was indeed the King of kings—but don't forget He was also a real human being.

Luke the doctor recorded that the Son of God was truly *born,* and wrapped in cloths and placed in a manger (Luke 2:7).

When He was eight days old the baby was circumcised (2:21) and then cuddled in an old man's arms (2:28).

123

He grew as a child (2:40,52), and once as a twelve-year-old He got separated from His parents and scolded (2:41-48), although His reason showed His growing awareness of His specialness and mission (2:49).

As an adult He got hungry (4:2); He shared human sadness (7:13); He liked to eat and drink and socialize with people (7:34). He wasn't omnipresent— He could only be in one place at a time (10:1).

And He died a real death (23:46) and ended His earthly life as He began it: wrapped in cloths and placed not in a manger but a tomb (23:52-53).

Think about this earthly, human, thirty-three-year life-span.

Jesus spent six times as long working as a carpenter as He did in full-time ministry. He was essentially a blue-collar worker, and that was His identification (Mark 6:3).

And I want to tell you—*it was a good thing He didn't shrink from all those laborious, tedious carpenter-years as His preparation.*

Once the ministry began . . .

> Never in human history were human
> frame and nervous system to be called on
> to endure such unremitting strain. . . . Only
> a physically perfect constitution could
> have supported such unceasing activity
> and expenditure of nervous force. . . .
>
> His recorded journeys during the three
> years covered at least two thousand five

> hundred miles on foot, frequently sur-
> rounded by crowds, and always teaching,
> preaching, healing.
>
> And what better preparation than twelve
> hours a day spent in the sawpit or at the
> bench, planing and hammering? These
> silent years . . . were invaluable in building
> up the physical and nervous reserves
> which were to be so heavily overdrawn in
> coming days that He would stagger under
> the weight of His cross.[18]

Jesus—pale, puffy-eyed, and effeminate, as in some of our paintings? No way. He was a "man's man."

And since His entrance into this world as a human, He will never cease to be a human!

In His risen manhood He assured the disciples He wasn't a ghost—and He said, "Touch Me and see." And He ate a piece of broiled fish in front of them (Luke 24:39-42).

Now in heaven there is a Man—the God-Man—at the Father's right hand! He's our go-between:

> There is one God and one mediator
> between God and men, the man Christ
> Jesus (1 Timothy 2:5).

And just as He was gloriously resurrected, we too, will be gloriously raised up:

> And just as we have borne the likeness of
> the earthly man [Adam], so shall we bear

the likeness of the man from heaven
[Christ] (1 Corinthians 15:49).

I can hardly wait, can you?

Still, we'll always know the price He paid to get us there. He'll be the only One there with scars in His hands.

Turn your eyes to Jesus—your strong Hero, your Ideal, your Model.

Let's pray together . . .

Lord, I look at You, and I discover You're looking at me!

"As in water face answers to face, so the heart of one man answers to another" (Proverbs 27:19, Berkeley).

You are like me—but perfect. You're all I want to be— but You're made of my kind of stuff. I can identify with You; I can move in close and be Your friend.

> *What an honor! What a thrill!*

> *You have said, "He who walks with the wise grows wise" (Proverbs 13:20).*

Lord Jesus Christ, I want to walk with You and grow to be like You. I fix my eyes on You, my wonderful Companion!

In Your dear name, amen.

A parting Glance

Ecce Homo—see the Man.
  Ecce Deum—see your God.
"Veiled in flesh, the Godhead see;
  Hail th' incarnate Deity"!

NINETEEN

Understanding Jesus, the Son of God

There's a very old cartoon by H.T. Webster entitled "Life in Harden County [Illinois] in 1809." It shows two men talking.

"Any news, Ezzie?"

"Squire McClendon's gone down to Washington to see Harding sworn in."

"I hear Bonaparte's trying to subdue Spain."

"New baby boy born down the street at the Lincolns'. Nothin' exciting ever happens around here."

Yet of course something exciting *had* happened: That new little life would one day reshape American history.

But the first Christmas produced the most dramatic event of all: The Son of God was born on our planet—in a part of His process to resolve all human history from start to finish.

> Out of the ivory palaces into a world of
> woe;
> Only His great, eternal love made my
> Savior go.

He had always, eternally, been alive and active. "In the beginning was the Word," says John 1:1—reaching back beyond creation, before Genesis 1:1!

Just as His death was not the end of Him, so His birth was not the beginning of Him.[19]

He was God. And yet He came to this world and "made himself nothing . . . being made in human likeness" (Philippians 2:7).

Incredible! He created everything—and then He voluntarily submitted to His own creation! He became tired and thirsty, just like one of us. Before, He'd been so furious against sin that He refused at first to lead His people into the Promised Land: He said they were so rebellious, He "might destroy [them] on the way" (Exodus 33:3).

Yet descending to earth, He stooped so far down that He meekly asked a prostitute for a drink of water.

Truly, profoundly, *"He humbled himself"* (Philippians 2:8).

Jesus was a man—but *don't ever forget He was and is God.*

Centuries before He came, Isaiah had predicted that a child would be born, a Son would be given, with these magnificent names:

> Wonderful Counselor, Mighty God,
> Everlasting Father, Prince of Peace
> (Isaiah 9:6).

After His return to heaven, superstitions sprouted about just what His nature really was. And Colossians was written to say, "Look, people, get it straight: Jesus Christ isn't a maxi-angel, He isn't a mini-God—"

> He is the image of the invisible God, the firstborn over all creation. For by him all things were created . . .
> by him and for him. He is before all things, and in him all things hold together. . . .
>
> God was pleased to have all his fullness dwell in him (Colossians 1:15-19).

In Zechariah 13:6-7, God the Father calls the Messiah His "Associate" (NASB), His Fellow, His Equal.

In Isaiah 40:10 Christ is called "Jehovah," a name so glorious the Hebrews left out its vowels—"YHWH," making it unpronounceable. And whenever a scribe copying Scriptures wrote out that name, he would first wipe his pen and dip it in fresh ink.

This is our Holy One, Jesus Christ the Lord, the Son of God.

When Peter called Him this—"the Christ, the Son of the living God"—Jesus answered, "Blessed are you" (Matthew 16:16-17).

John told all his readers it was the reason he wrote his book:

> That you may believe that Jesus is the
> Christ, the Son of God, and that by
> believing you may have life in his name
> (John 20:31).

Is your heart right now bowed in acknowledgment? And are your eyes focused on Him?

Let's pray together...

Lord, I say with Job,
"My ears had heard of you
but now my eyes have seen you"
(Job 42:5).
And I say with Thomas,
"My Lord and my God!" (John 20:28).

A parting Glance

The night was long, and the shadows
  spread
As far as the eye could see;
I stretched my hands to a human Christ,
And He walked through the dark with me!
Out of the dimness at last we came,
Our feet on the dawn-warmed sod;
And I saw by the light of His wondrous
  eyes
I walked with the Son of God.

—HARRIET WARD BEECHER

TWENTY

Understanding Jesus, The Crucified One

If you've ever been the victim of an action that's blatantly unfair, consider Jesus. Acquitted by the highest court of the land ("I find no basis for a charge against him," John 19:4,6), He is led away and roughly nailed to a cross to die anyway!

Even in this crisis, the habit of His life continues: He prays. "Father, forgive them. . . ."

Who is "them"?

Not just the Gentile soldiers carrying out the act.

Not just the Jewish mob shouting, "Let His blood be on us and on our children!"

Father, forgive all people from Adam on: "All have sinned." All are responsible for His death.

Forgive *me*, Anne Ortlund.

Forgive *you*, reader.

". . . for they do not know what they are
doing." You didn't know; I didn't know—
we weren't even born yet!

Remember the Old Testament Israelites who qualified to live in one of the Cities of Refuge because
they'd accidentally killed somebody? We're like that.
We crucified Jesus "unintentionally and without
malice aforethought" (Joshua 20:5).

Nevertheless, we did it: We killed Him. We
sinned—and to pay for us, He had to die.

Wrote Johann Heerman in about 1630—and he
was right—

> Who was the guilty? Who brought this
>   upon Thee?
> Alas, my treason, Jesus, hath undone
>   Thee!
> 'Twas I, Lord Jesus, I it was denied Thee:
> I crucified Thee.

And it was so terrible, when it happened all
nature went bonkers. From high noon to mid-after-
noon, a thick blanket of darkness covered everything.
An earthquake rattled the land so violently that rocks
split. Tombs broke open, and people long dead got up
and walked out of their graves and into the city!

The walls of the temple were left undamaged—
and yet inside, the great thirty-by-sixty-foot curtain
separating the Holy Place (where humans could go)
from the Most Holy Place (where dwelt the presence

of God) was split right down the middle—interestingly, from the top to the bottom.

"Surely this man was the Son of God!" said one soldier (Mark 15:39). There was no other explanation. And yet—

> The scandal of the incarnation . . . [is] the shame of a God who has so wallowed in the muck and misery of the world that He has become indistinguishable from it.[20]

> When we shall see him, there is no beauty that we should desire him. He is despised and rejected of men; a man of sorrows, and acquainted with grief: and we hid as it were our faces from him; he was despised, and we esteemed him not (Isaiah 53:2-3 KJV).

> By Thy sweat bloody and clotted! Thy soul in agony,
> Thy head crowned with thorns, bruised with staves,
> Thine eyes a fountain of tears,
> Thine ears full of insults,
> Thy mouth moistened with vinegar and gall,
> Thy face stained with spitting,
> Thy neck bowed down with the burden of the cross,
> Thy back ploughed with the wheals and wounds
>   of the scourge,
> Thy pierced hands and feet,
> Thy strong cry, Eli, Eli,
> Thy heart pierced with the spear,
> The water and blood thence flowing,
> Thy body broken, Thy blood poured out—
> Lord forgive the iniquity of Thy servant
> And cover all his sin.[21]

The Lancelot Andrewes quotation above was to end this chapter. But when I'd written these words I got down on my face on the floor.

I groaned, "O God, O God! Have I written this chapter hoping I've written 'powerfully' to touch people about Your crucifixion—so they'd buy the book and I'd make money? Am I standing near the cross hawking my wares to take advantage of the Great Event?

"Then I'm another Demetrius!" (You remember him, the silversmith in Acts 19:24. He lived under the shadow of the great goddess idol Artemis, and he didn't want Christ preached because he made a good income selling little silver shrines to the tourists who came to worship her.)

Oh, a thousand, thousand curses on all Demetriuses!

I, too, bow myself at Jesus' cross, in humility and shame. I repent of all my personal sin that put Him there.

You do the same.

O Lord, Lord! Forgive us our dry eyes.

TWENTY ONE

Understanding Jesus, The Risen One

When I'm finished speaking somewhere I can easily worry, "Did I come across too bossy? Did I come across too unfeeling and hard-nosed? Did I put anybody down? Did I offend? Did I intimidate? Did I act like the big know-it-all?" and so on, and so on—and I agonize. When I start thinking that way, *my eyes are on myself*. When that happens, I need to turn my eyes to our risen Lord. His resurrection makes all the difference in my life—and yours. That's where everything changes!

1. Because of His resurrection He offers you His presence.

In His earthly body Jesus could only be in one place at one time (Luke 10:1). But that wasn't the case with His resurrection body: "On the evening of that first day of the week, when the disciples were together, with the doors locked for fear of the Jews, Jesus came and stood among them" (John 20:19).

Because our Jesus is risen and omnipresent, I can say, "Lord, help me to refocus my eyes on You. I committed all this to You before I began. I believe You took charge, and that You covered all my humanness that would have distracted from You." And I put that session in my two hands and surrender it to Him again.

At His birth He was given two names: "Jesus" (Matthew 1:21) and "Immanuel" (Matthew 1:22-23). "Jesus" means "Savior," and He was called that all His earthly life.

But "Immanuel" means "God with us," and it's more appropriate now than ever. Standing on the mountain in His resurrection body, ready to go back to heaven, Jesus said, "I am with you always" (Matthew 28:20).

He is with you right now, as you read this. Are your eyes on Him?

> The light of Christ surrounds you.
> The love of Christ enfolds you.
> The power of Christ protects you.
> The presence of Christ watches over you.
> Wherever you are, Christ is.

2. *Because of His resurrection, He offers you His peace.* Said the newly risen Christ, "Peace be with you!" (John 20:19-20).

Shalom, the Hebrew word for peace, means wholeness, health, well-being, not only outside but inside.

Christ is here, it's okay. Peace. In the midst of your problems, it's okay. Peace.

And when Jesus said, "Shalom"—or "salaam"—He wasn't just saying, "Hi, have a nice day." He was bestowing His peace. Will you believe that? Will you discipline your heart to take what He offers?

> Thou wilt keep him in perfect peace,
> whose mind is stayed on thee (Isaiah 26:3,
> KJV—or "whose eyes are fixed on You"!).

Now may the Lord of peace himself give you peace at all times and in every way (2 Thessalonians 3:16).

3. *Because of His resurrection He offers you His purpose.*

One of the first things Jesus said in His resurrection body was this: "As the Father has sent me, I am sending you" (John 20:21).

A brand new principle was suddenly at work!

Back in His earthly life He'd often say, in essence, "Now, don't tell anyone about Me" (Mark 1:43; 3:12; 5:43; 7:36; 8:30; and so on). From our side of the resurrection, that seems absolutely strange.

But when Christ exploded out of that grave, all His followers exploded into action. "Go!" He said. "Tell! Be My witnesses to the ends of earth!" (*see* Matthew 28:19; Acts 1:8).

The resurrection not only changed *Him,* it changed *them.* Boy, did they go! Apparently only one of the apostles died in his homeland. They went everywhere, and "preached the word wherever they went" (Acts 8:4). Acts is the book of action.

His new purpose was now their new purpose.

His new life was their new life.

They were now in Him, and He was now in them.

Jesus' resurrection—it meant everything! He's risen; He's alive!

Fix your eyes on Him: What's He telling you to do? Then go for it!

4. *Because of His resurrection He offers you His power.* I can't tell you how the fact of Jesus Christ's power encourages me and motivates me. When I speak or write, there's no strength in me to do it on my own.

How could there be? Hey, when I interact with my children or go on a date with Ray, there's no strength in me to do it on my own! I'd bungle into arguing or getting critical of someone, or I might be just dull and boring. In myself, I wouldn't have the words to bless or lift or even be fun.

Let me give you here a very important truth for your living: *Your weaknesses—totally acknowledged and continually realized—give you your only claim and access to His resurrection power.*

I've been a Christian since I was about six years old, and I don't think I'm any stronger now than when I was six. And it's all right with me.

Are you weak? The Lord doesn't take that weakness away. He says, "My power is made perfect in weakness" (2 Corinthians 12:9).

And Paul's response to this was,

> Therefore I will boast all the more gladly
> about my weaknesses, so that Christ's
> power may rest upon me. . . . When I am
> weak, then I am strong (2 Corinthians
> 12:9-10).

Don't be concerned or embarrassed over your weaknesses. Don't try to forget them or hide them or pray to conquer them or be freed from them.

Jesus doesn't *make you stronger*. The risen Lord said, "You will receive power when the Holy Spirit comes upon you" (Acts 1:8). It's His power only; it always has been, always will be. He doesn't lessen your weaknesses and add a little of His strength, the way I blend a glass of iced tea.

Your total weakness and His total strength are to coexist side by side.

> We have this treasure in jars of clay to
> show that this all-surpassing power is from
> God and not from us (2 Corinthians 4:7).

In all your struggles and temptations, turn your eyes on the resurrected Jesus! Let the only measure of your expectations for yourself be the power of Jesus Christ.

Then you can live a truly powerful life—not because you're no longer weak, but because, being weak, you count on His power to work in you.

We had company for dinner the other night, and the two lamps flanking the couch wouldn't go on. After our friends had left, Ray investigated and found the plug in the wall socket was sort of sagging out and had lost its connection.

Never mind your weaknesses; just make sure you're solidly connected, strongly "abiding in Him."

Then expect the power of His resurrection to work in your life.

> With that he breathed on them and said,
> "Receive the Holy Spirit" (John 20:22).

Right now, sit loose in your chair.

Breathe out—I'm doing it, too—as if expelling your lack of confidence in His abilities on your behalf.

Now prayerfully breathe in, in a sense, a fresh filling of His Holy Spirit. Breathe in new expectations of His victories in your life.

Turn your eyes on Jesus.

Let's pray together . . .

O wonderful Lord Jesus Christ of the empty tomb,
I receive anew Your presence.
I receive anew Your peace.
I receive anew Your purpose.
I receive anew Your power.
In Your own dear name, amen.

"Look to the Lord and his strength"
  (Psalm 105:4).

Looking at Jesus will infuse your
  life with power.
Looking much at Jesus will infuse
  your life with much power.
Looking continually at Jesus will
  infuse your life with continual
  power.

TWENTY TWO

Understanding Jesus, the Eternal One

The "Ancient of Days," Daniel called Him.

Take a long, hard look at Jesus Christ in the far-away past. . . back, back, back. . . .

Back before creation, the Father had loved Him (John 17:24).

Back before the world began, He shared the Father's glory (John 17:5), and with Him made all things (Colossians 1:16).

He declares, speaking as our Wisdom (1 Corinthians 1:30),

> I was there when he set the heavens in place . . . and when he marked out the foundations of the earth. Then was I the

craftsman at his side (Proverbs
8:27,29,30).

God in Christ separated light from darkness,
   separated water above from water below,
   separated seas from dry ground.

God in Christ ordered the ground to fill up with
         seeds producing vegetation,
   the waters to fill up with fish,
   the land to fill up with animals and insects.

Then *God in Christ* commanded the plants and
         creatures to die,
   their bodies to fall back into the ground, their
         remains to compress and become coal,
         diamonds, oil, gas—vast, vast reserves of
         natural resources probably not all discov-
         ered even yet.

Why?

All these lived not for themselves but for us. God
in Christ was forming them long ago to heat winters
they would never live through, to light buildings they
would never see.

*God in Christ, with infinite wisdom and skill and love,
was preparing a place for us.* (The Ancient of Days, the
Eternal One, loved us even back then.)

Yet by our sin, we've been destroying the place He
prepared.

How sad God must have been to have to tell Adam, "Because you listened to your wife and ate . . . cursed is the ground" (Genesis 3:17)!

And ever since then,

> We know that the whole creation has been groaning as in the pains of childbirth right up to the present time (Romans 8:22).
> The earth dries up and withers. . . .
> The earth is defiled by its people;
>   they have disobeyed the laws.
> Therefore a curse consumes the earth
> (Isaiah 24:4-6).

A woman once exclaimed to her famous pastor, Dr. Charles Spurgeon, "Oh, Dr. Spurgeon, I'm afraid the world is coming to an end!"

"Never mind, my dear," he said; "we can get along without it." That's the good news!

Jesus knew all along what we would do with the wonderful place He gave us, His gift prepared with such love and skill—and He's getting a replacement ready:

> Do not let your hearts be troubled. . . . In my Father's house are many rooms. . . . I am going there to prepare a place for you (John 14:1-2).

He's preparing a second place for us in our resurrection, perfection, glory!

If this first place was so beautiful and so equipped, what will the new one be like? Jesus hasn't forgotten you; He has you in His heart. He's been getting another place ready, and He says, "I am making everything new!" (Revelation 21:5).

Look upon Jesus, and you'll stumble on wonder after wonder—and every wonder will be true.

Now take a long, hard at Jesus in the future.

> Then every creature will be singing, To him who sits on the throne and to the Lamb be praise and honor and glory and power, for ever and ever! (Revelation 5:13).

Surely you'll want to bow your knees to pray to such a One,

Lord, I'm "lost in wonder, love, and praise."

Lord, You have told me that You know the plans You have for me, plans to prosper me and not to harm me, plans to give me hope and a future (Jeremiah 29:11).

I can hardly wait.

Lord, I look at Your eternal past and I see it marred by our sin. But I look at Your eternal future—and my eternal future with You—and my heart leaps.

Even so, come, Lord Jesus.

Amen and amen.

Thou great I AM,
Fill my mind with elevation and grandeur
    at the thought of a Being
    with whom one day is as a thousand
        years,
        and a thousand years as one day,
A mighty God who, amidst the lapse of
        worlds,
    and the revolutions of empires,
    feels no variableness,
    but is glorious in immortality.
May I rejoice that, while men die, the
        Lord lives;
    that, while all creatures are broken
        reeds,
        empty cisterns,
        fading flowers,
        withering grass,
    he is the rock of ages,
        the fountain of living waters.

—OLD PURITAN PRAYER

TWENTY THREE

Understanding Jesus, the Returning Lord

At that electrifying point in time, nobody will have to be told anymore. Every eye in the universe will be focused on Jesus. Says Revelation 1:7,

> Look, he is coming with the clouds, and
> every eye will see him, even those who
> pierced him; and all peoples of the earth
> will mourn because of him.

What a shock! At that moment millions will be begging, "Wait! Wait, I'm not ready!"

But *time will have stopped.*

And the Spirit will never again plead, "Today, if you hear his voice, do not harden your hearts" (Hebrews 4:7).

There'll be no more "today"!

Suddenly, every person will be caught in his tracks. Like action on television, in an instant the frame will freeze! And then this verse will come true:

> Let him who does wrong continue to do
> wrong;
> Let him who is vile continue to be vile;
> Let him who does right continue to do right,
> And let him who is holy continue to be holy
>
> (REVELATION 22:11).

And it will be judgment time.

The other day I was carelessly tootling along in the car doing 65 in a 55-mile-per-hour zone, and not even conscience-stricken because all the cars around me were going at least that fast.

But suddenly at the side of the road was a brand-new gadget our City of Newport Beach had just installed: It recorded my personal speed—only mine—in huge numbers for all the world to see. Newport Beach with all its powers of authority and punishment was scrutinizing me—at that moment only lil' ol' me. I tell you, I felt guilty as sin. My heart raced as I slowed down to 55 and looked in my mirror for the Long Arm of the Law. There wasn't any. Whew.

But that is nothing compared with the moment when the Lord Jesus as Judge will fix His eye on me:

> We must all appear before the judgment
> seat of Christ, that each one may receive
> what is due him for the things done while

in the body, whether good or bad (2 Corinthians 5:10).

That's why 1 John 2:28 says, "Dear children, *continue* [or abide] *in him*, so that when he appears, we may be confident and unashamed before him at his coming" (emphasis added).

Just the same, consider these wonderful facts:

1. He loves us! (1 John 3:1).
2. We're going to be like Him! (1 John 3:2).

When at His return He wants to so gloriously transform you— don't you dare take advantage of that promise and fool around now. You'd be so embarrassed, so full of regrets!

Everyone who has this hope in him *purifies himself* (1 John 3:3, emphasis added).

Let's pray together . . .

O Lord God, we have all eternity to enjoy our rewards, as Amy Carmichael said, and only a few short years to win them.

Lord, write eternity on my eyeballs. May I see all things from Your perspective—and most of all, may I see You Yourself.

> *O Lord, I want to live at this moment,*
> *and the rest of this day,*
> *and the rest of my life,*

so that I can continually say, "Come, Lord
Jesus! Come soon! Come now!"
I want to see You, Lord.
In Your precious name, amen.

Lord of the cloud and fire,
I am a stranger, with a stranger's
    indifference;
My hands hold a pilgrim's staff,
My march is Zionward,
My eyes are toward the coming of
    the Lord.

—OLD PURITAN PRAYER

PART FIVE

Looking to Jesus for a Clear Focus

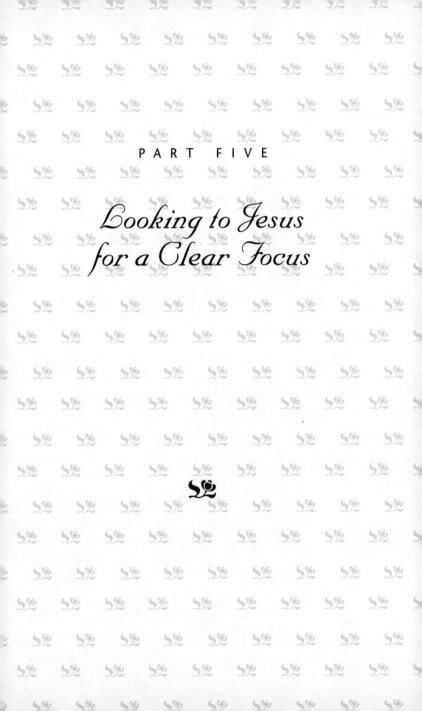

*Oh, fix our earnest gaze
So wholly, Lord, on You,
That with Your beauty occupied
All else is dimmer view.*

Jesus

Focusing on Jesus
and Nothing Else

As you're reading this book page right now, your eyes are focused only on the print. You're somewhat aware of your arms,

> your lap,
> your chair,
> your surroundings

—aware enough that you wouldn't suddenly move so that you'd bump against something; aware enough that you'd know if a dog or a person suddenly arrived on the scene. So although your peripheral vision is a safeguard, a buffer zone, it doesn't occupy your immediate attention.

Are you living your life like that? When you fix your eyes on Jesus your focus will be on Him. You don't need to focus on the other matters of life, for your peripheral vision will be enough to take care of them.

Hebrews 12:2 is our theme verse in this book: "Let us fix our eyes on Jesus." Unfortunately, there's a meaning in the original words that's lost in most translations: the verse speaks of looking *away* to Jesus with such concentration that you don't see anything else quite as clearly.

"Away": that's the untranslated adverb.

I remember a time when I was going to travel to Texas on "book business." It had been a while since I'd had time to think about my wardrobe, and a week before I left for Texas, God brought it to my mind.

Around the edges of my consciousness He planted the thought, *You need a couple of dresses for Texas and for summer church and conference speaking.*

A day or two later I was sitting in a restaurant engrossed in eating lunch, reading my Bible, and writing my prayers. Afterward as I turned to go I realized that next door was a women's clothing shop. I remembered my need, and there in plain view were two simple summer dresses: my size, my price, my autumn colors. On the spot I got them, with shoes for one and earrings for the other, and I knew that what I already had at home would finish the two outfits. Thank you, Abba Father. . . .

It will probably be a year before I need to get any more summer clothes.

Now, sometimes my life isn't that smooth and efficient. Sometimes God allows hassles in my life; He knows when I need them to grow. He's so kind!

But as a general rule for living, Matthew 6:33 will always be true: "Seek first his kingdom and his righteousness, and dresses, shoes, and earrings will be given to you as well." Right?

No, that's not quite how the verse goes: "*All these things*"—whatever is needed to help you live while you "seek first."

The point is, *look away to Jesus.*

Let's pray together . . .

> Heavenly Father, may the focus of my life be—
> > *not on myself* (page 165)
> > *not on others* (page 167)
> > *not on my troubles* (page 173)
> > *not on material things* (page 177)
> > *not on the devil* (page 181)
> > *not on ugliness* (page 189)
>
> Help me to look away from all these to Jesus!
> In His worthy name, amen.

TWENTY FIVE

Focusing on Jesus and Not Yourself

You get no forgiveness from just looking at all your sins.

You get no healing from concentrating on your diseases.

You get no redemption from studying the pit you're in.

You get no crowning with glory from fixing your eyes on your failures.

You get no fulfillment of desires from looking at all you don't have.

You get no renewal from focusing on your old-ness, staleness, dryness.

Only He

> forgives all your sins . . .
> heals all your diseases . . .

redeems your life from the pit . . .
crowns you with love and compassion . . .
satisfies your desires with good things,
so that your youth is renewed like the
eagle's (Psalm 103:3-5).

Only He!

Look to yourself, and ultimately you'll be embarrassed. But:

> Those who look to him are radiant; their
> faces are never covered with shame (Psalm
> 34:5).

Let's pray together . . .

Lord, I'm ready to be radiant.

You know my battle! You know how often my attention is on myself. Then I'm shut up, as Malcolm Muggeridge says, in the dark prison of my own ego.

Lord Jesus, I fix my eyes on You.

I come out into radiant sunshine; I'm walking in the light! But may my joy not be in the light as much as in You.

For Your own dear sake, amen.

Focusing on Jesus and Not Others

Let me tell you how this truth recently hit home to me.

Sometimes Ray and I—and so do you—see generations slip. You see

> a husband and wife going hard after
>   the Lord;
> their children attending church more
>   often that not;
> and their grandchildren totally uninter-
>   ested in spiritual things.

And through the years we've prayed, "Lord, keep the fire hot! Keep our children fervent for You, our grandchildren fervent for You, our great grandchildren. . . ." And God, out of His amazing grace and not because we're deserving, has been answering our prayers.

So you can understand our thrill when the first grandchild, Lisa, so zealous for God, became engaged to wonderful Mark, who loves Him as much as she does.

It's with much prayer that I tell you what I've said so far, saying, "Lord, don't let this be bragging! So many godly parents have rebellious children, and we're no better."

But I tell you the next part of the story with even more prayer, knowing I'm opening myself up for attack.

Help me, Jesus.

By the night of the wedding I was giddy with joy. God was so faithful to hear our prayers; Lisa and Mark were such treasures. Pastors Ray and John, grandfather and father of the bride, performed the ceremony before all John's loving congregation.

("... Who gives this woman to be married to this man?"

"Your daughter and I do. ..." We choked with laughter and tears.)

At the reception (filled with the Spirit but no "spirits"), the little band began a happy beat, and Ray and I were too exhilarated to sit still any longer. We don't know how to dance, but we were silly enough that night to discover we could wiggle without touching with the best of them. I hoofed around with

Ray, with son Nels, and with a teenage Iranian boy our grandson had just led to know Christ.

(Some readers are reacting, "Yea for the grandson! Yea for the new believer!" And some are reacting, "Boo for corrupting a new Christian!" Help me, Lord.)

Neither Nels nor the new friend knew any more about dancing than we did, but it was celebration time, and we were all exuberant.

At a break in the festivities, a young woman came up to me and said, "I'm from northern California, and my small group and I have been so blessed studying your book *Discipling One Another.* May I take your picture?"

Suddenly I came to and thought, *Dear Lord, what has she been watching? I wouldn't for the world offend another Christian.*

I thought of Romans 14 and the need to live conservatively for others' sakes.

Then I thought, The bride's *grandmother?* Gimme a break.

Then I thought of David's uninhibited happiness in 2 Samuel 6, and, like him, I said to myself, "It was before the Lord. . . ."

In telling you this, reader, I'm exposed and vulnerable, and I'm humbly asking God to cover me from criticisms, for His sake. I tell it to you not to "justify dancing"—horrors, no—but because I learned again on Lisa's wedding night that *interior motives,* not *exterior actions,* are the bottom line.

> The Lord does not look at the things
> man looks at. Man looks at the outward
> appearance, but the Lord looks at the heart
> (1 Samuel 16:7).

When He sees a rebellious heart, even that man's *plowing* is sin (Proverbs 21:4); he can't do *anything* right.

But this whole issue of "What's right? What's wrong?" is the reason for Romans 14, and the point of it is this: Fix your eyes not on others, but on Jesus.

Never mind what other Christians do or don't do; "to his own master [not to you or me] he stands or falls" (Romans 14:4). "Therefore let us stop passing judgment on one another" (verse 13).

"Whatever we do, let's do it *to the Lord*," says Romans 14. "And whatever we decide *not* to do, let's abstain *to the Lord*."

All eyes directed up!

It's a dumb kind of Christianity that constantly looks sideways to check out what each other is doing. It will make us clean the outside of the cup while inside we may be full of wickedness (Luke 11:39): deceit, criticisms, and outward show.

Don't fix your eyes on others.

Fix your eyes on Jesus alone, and give Him pleasure.

Let's pray together . . .

How different Your flowers are, O blessed Creator, how different Your insects, how different Your sea creatures, how different Your children!

O Spirit of God, clothe me with compassion, kindness, humility, gentleness, and patience. May I bear with others, forgive others, truly love others.

And most of all, may I fix my eyes on Jesus.

In His own name, amen.

Guy King says that there's a gold running cup on another man's mantel that could have been—should have been—on his own.

He was running toward the tape, coming in number one.

Somebody was trailing on his right, and he shot a look to see where he was. It was the split-second distraction that his competitor needed, and he flashed by him and won.

"Our sole safety [as Christians]," says Guy King, "is to be found in keeping our eyes averted . . . from others, and keeping them unswervingly 'looking unto Jesus.'"

—BROUGHT IN, PP. 72-73

Focusing on Jesus and Not Your Troubles

I look to Thee in every need
And never look in vain;
I feel Thy strong and tender love
And all is well again:
The thought of Thee is mightier far
Than sin and pain and sorrow are.

—SAMUEL LONGFELLOW

"Sin and pain and sorrow"—all your troubles—are so limited and weak, they're not worthy of your full concentration.

Your troubles can't shut off the power of God's Spirit to work on your behalf.

They can't change His long-range plans for you.

They can't thwart the ability of His Word to comfort and direct you.

They can't lessen the availability of your Christian brothers and sisters to encourage you.

They can't reduce your eternal life!

Then don't let them overcome you.

Fix your eyes on Jesus, and ask Him for godly optimism, steadiness, endurance.

Take courage from Psalm 25:15:

> My eyes are ever on the Lord, for only he
> will release my feet from the snare.

Let's pray together . . .

Dear Lord God, thank You for giving me my troubles! First Peter 1:7 says that You've given them to prove that my faith is genuine, when it gets refined in these fires; and that they will result in praise, glory, and honor to You.

Then, Lord, I don't fix my eyes on my troubles but on You. I offer You my praise, glory, and honor! I'm so happy that these very trials are proving that my faith is in You and I trust You.

Alleluia!

In Christ's dear name, amen.

A parting Glance

For every one look at your problems,
your weaknesses, your failures—
take ten looks at Jesus.

—ROBERT MURRAY McCHEYNE,
FIERY SCOTTISH PREACHER
WHO DIED AT THE AGE
OF TWENTY-NINE

TWENTY EIGHT

Focusing on Jesus and Not Material Things

Here's a nineteenth-century person riding along in his carriage on a dark but star-lit night, says Søren Kierkegaard, as paraphrased by Anne Ortlund.

He's got all his coach lights on, so as he drives along he can see in front of him just fine. But with those strong lights all around him he can't see the stars very well—in the same way that, if you're a materialist, you can't see Jesus very well.

Now, says Kierkegaard, on this dark but starlit night here comes a poor peasant. He has no carriage and no lights at all, so you'd think he'd get a glorious view of the stars. The only problem is, he's probably so busy looking down to make sure he doesn't fall in a hole, he doesn't see the stars, either.

Similarly, if you get rid of every single material possession, just the business of living would certainly be more awkward, and probably be so distracting and consuming that you wouldn't fix your eyes on Jesus, either. Asceticism is no answer.

So the big question is: How many lanterns do you need? How many material things are just enough to live efficiently and yet still have a good sight of Jesus?

The "good life" isn't achieved by gross consumption of material goods. (Do you know that the word *miser,* which means "one who hoards," and the word *misery* come from exactly the same root?)

But neither is "the good life" achieved by the least possible consumption of material goods. Says Vernard Eller,

> The point is that these things can be good—very good—if they are used to support man's relationship to God rather than compete with it.[22]

As I write these words I'm shut off from the phone and all activities, in the total quiet of a kind friend's beach condo, his "second home." At this moment it's a lantern to light my way to see how to write this book. My friend is using his condo not to "compete with God" but to "support man's relationship to Him." And I know his heart as well as I know my own—that we both want to keep our lives dark enough to see the stars.

Nobody can tell you how many lanterns you personally need, and don't judge anyone else's decisions. Simply keep your own lanterns few enough so that most of all, you can see Him!

> Turn your eyes upon Jesus,
>> Look full in His wonderful face;
> And the things of earth will grow strangely
>> dim
>> In the light of His glory and grace.[23]

Let's pray together...

Open my eyes, Lord; I want to see Jesus,
To reach out and touch Him and say
that I love Him.
Open my ears, Lord; please help me to listen.
Open my eyes, Lord; I want to see Jesus. *

---

* Words and music by Bob Cull. Copyright 1976 by Maranatha Music, Box 1396, Costa Mesa, California 92626.

TWENTY NINE

Focusing on Jesus and Not the Enemy

Spiritual warfare is the latest "game" some Christians are trying to play, for several reasons. Think about it.

There are three major negative influences to blame for all our troubles: the world, the flesh, and the devil.

Many Christians really like *the world* these days. They're fascinated by it, they're cozying up to it, they're copying it. So they're saying—perhaps unconsciously—"Let's not blame the world for our problems. We might have to back off from it."

And many Christians are trying hard to like *the flesh*. They think putting it down would damage their self-image. So they're saying—not in actual words—"Let's not blame the flesh; that would be blaming *me*."

("If I can wriggle out of responsibility and blame all my ills on an external force out there, it takes 'me' off the hook.")

So let's blame *the devil!* I really didn't want to do that—"the devil made me do it."

Perhaps another reason we play "spiritual warfare" is because it's sensational. Teaching about it is exciting; it raises a flap; it's cops and robbers on a universal scale.

Unfortunately, an amazing number of Christians these days are full of fear rather than faith—because their eyes are fixed on the devil, not on Jesus.

When I was about five, a bigger neighbor girl would get hold of me and put me in a dark room and tell me ghost stories. One day she told me about the Red Hands. She said they were out to get me and that I wasn't safe a minute.

I took off!

I walked for miles before Daddy, out scouting in his car, found me and brought me home again.

But for weeks after that, I wouldn't go into a dark room alone; somebody had to precede me and turn on the lights first. (This was before switches were by the door.)

And to get into my bed I'd make a mighty leap so the Red Hands under my bed couldn't grab my ankles. I was a mess.

The difference between the Red Hands and the devil is that *the devil is real.*

First Peter 5:8 warns, "Be self-controlled and alert. Your enemy the devil prowls around like a roaring lion looking for someone to devour."

Then shouldn't we be constantly terrified, like little Anne Sweet?

C. S. Lewis wrote:

> There are two equal and opposite errors into which our race can fall about the devils. One is to disbelieve in their existence. The other is to believe, and to feel and excessive and unhealthy interest in them.[24]

Are you fixing your eyes on the devil? I hear you're never supposed to make eye contact with an unfamiliar—especially an unfriendly—dog; he takes that as a threat.

Well, don't get over-occupied with Satan, either. Martin Luther wrote,

> One does not gain much ground against the devil with a lengthy disputation; but with brief words and replies, such as: "I am a Christian, of the same flesh and blood as is my Lord Christ, the Son of God. Settle your accounts with Him." Then the devil does not stay long.

I have a better idea. (Who am I to improve on Martin Luther?!) *Don't talk to him at all.* Jude says that fools are those who

> . . . slander celestial beings. But even the
> archangel Michael, when he was disputing
> with the devil about the body of Moses,
> did not dare bring a slanderous accusation
> against [the devil], but said, "The Lord
> rebuke you!" (verses 8-9).

The devil is too dangerous, too "un-understood," too powerful for us to stand up and try to eyeball him. I don't know, maybe he thinks it's just plain hilarious when you or I try to "rebuke" him; even the great Michael didn't dare to.

I notice in Zechariah 3 that when the devil was hassling Joshua the high priest—spiritually by far the most important man of that day—the Lord Himself rebuked the devil on behalf of Joshua.

So when you're in turmoil, what do you do?

First, seek to pin down the primary cause of your situation.

1. Is the world to blame?

Have you been "worldly"—involved with the world, secretly admiring it, copying its thinking, its lifestyle?

> Don't you know that friendship with the
> world is hatred toward God? (James 4:4)
> What fellowship can light have with
> darkness? . . .
> > "Therefore come out from them and be
> > > separate. . . .
> > Touch no unclean thing,
> > > and I will receive you" . . . says the Lord
> > > Almighty (2 Corinthians 6:14-18).

Repent of your fooling around; extricate yourself! Fix your eyes only on Jesus, and tell Him you want to love only Him.

2. *Is the flesh to blame?* Did you make bad choices? Should you yourself take responsibility for your trouble?

> Do not be deceived: God cannot be mocked. A man reaps what he sows. The one who sows to please his sinful nature [or flesh], from that [flesh] will reap destruction (Galatians 6:7-8).

Repent of what you did, or said, or thought, all by yourself. Let God forgive you and cleanse you totally—and then fix your eyes on Jesus.

3. *Is the devil to blame?* Ephesians 6 is the classic chapter on what to do about Satan. How do you struggle against "the powers of this dark world and against the spiritual forces of evil in the heavenly realms"? Ephesians 6 doesn't suggest a quick fix. Let's look.

First, the solution in Ephesians 6 is *preventative.* You start *now*, ahead of time: "Put on the full armor of God, so that when the day of evil comes, you may be able to stand your ground, and after you have done everything, to stand" (verse 13).

What, Lord? You mean to say we don't get to start right now whipping our sword around, and maybe like Peter cut off somebody's ear?

No, the Lord Himself will do your fighting for you; He's definitely more qualified. Your place is to *stand.*

Second, the solution in Ephesians 6 is *thorough:* "After you have done everything"!

What must you do? "Put on the full armor"—don't miss a single piece—of truth, righteousness, readiness that comes from the gospel, faith, salvation, and the Word of God; and through it all, praying always.

Put on every one of these:

1. *Salvation:* Make sure you're born again.

2. *The Word of God:* Get into a Bible class or a Bible correspondence course or some kind of instruction.

3. *Truth:* Learn right doctrine; expose yourself to good Bible preaching, good radio teaching.

4. *Prayer:* It's not easy but crucial: Keep a daily quiet time.

5. *Readiness that comes from the gospel:* Know what "the gospel," in a nutshell, really is—it's found, for instance, in 1 Corinthians 15:1-4—so you can share it.

6. *Righteousness:* Be careful to maintain moral integrity.

7. *Faith:* Trust yourself utterly to the Lord.

And third, the solution in Ephesians 6 is *positive!* This armor against the devil is an aggressively happy, good lifestyle.

Simply seek to live a diligent Christian life. That's the unsensational, steady, pleasant, poised, serene stance of power that will make the devil go bother somebody else.

> The prince of darkness grim,
> We tremble not for him!

Fix your eyes on Jesus—and you'll find yourself full of faith, not fear.

Let's pray together...

I reject the devil's influence in my life, O Lord. I ask You to rebuke him; I know the battle is Yours, and I am called only to stand firm. Lord, I fix my eyes on Jesus; I want to live aggressively in His disciplines.

Lord, clothe me with the perfection of your seven pieces of armor:

> *With truth,*
> *With righteousness,*
> *With the readiness that comes from the gospel,*
> *With faith,*
> *With salvation,*
> *With Your Word,*
> *And with prayer.*

In the strong name of the Lord Jesus Christ, amen.

✸

THIRTY

Focusing on Jesus and Not on Ugliness

I was sitting in the lounge of a Christian radio station, waiting my turn to go into the studio and guest a talk show. Another Christian program that was on the air at that moment was being intercommed into the lounge, so I couldn't help but listen.

It was gross.

In the name of "exposing" the sins of our day, shocking activities were being described, filthy words were being repeated. I guess listener reaction was supposed to be to pray or send money.

I thought about all the New Testament letters, which were written and circulated in an equally obscene world; the Roman culture was then in its last throes of degradation. But the Scriptures didn't describe the society's filth, they only warned against it.

The writers of Scripture focused on teaching the positive—both in doctrinal truth and practical application for daily living.

Never does Paul say Christians "need to be informed" of what they're fighting against so they can "pray intelligently." No, no! He says, "Stay ignorant!"

> Be wise about what is good, and innocent about what is evil (Romans 16:19).

> It is shameful even to mention what the disobedient do in secret (Ephesians 5:12).

How do you become "blameless and pure...in a crooked and depraved generation, in which you shine like stars in the universe" (Philippians 2:15)?

Philippians 4:8 tells you how:

> Whatever is true,
> whatever is noble,
> whatever is right,
> whatever is pure,
> whatever is lovely,
> whatever is admirable
> —if anything is excellent or praise-
> worthy—
> think about such things.

Surrounded by ugliness, think beauty.
Fix your eyes on Jesus.

Let's pray together . . .

O Lord Jesus Christ,
John saw You among the lampstands,

> with Your face shining like the sun in all its bril-
>   liance,
> and Your voice like the sound of rushing waters,
> and seven stars in Your right hand.

I can't imagine how beautiful You must be.

> A rainbow encircles You,
> and before You is a sea of glass...
>   an exquisitely pure reflecting pool...
>   doubling all Your splendor.
> I see flashes of lightning from your throne;
>   I hear exploding peals of thunder;
>   I smell heavenly incense from the
>   golden bowls....

My senses are dazzled.
Almost without breath, I'm lost in wonder, love, and
praise.
I fix my eyes on You.

PART SIX

Looking to Jesus Now and Always

To remember Thee, to worship Thee,
to confess to Thee, to praise Thee,
to bless Thee, to hymn Thee,
to give thanks to Thee,
maker, nourisher, guardian, governor,
preserver, worker, perfector of all,
Lord and Father,
King and God,
fountain of life and immortality,
treasure of everlasting goods,
whom the heavens hymn,
and the heaven of heavens,
the angels and all the heavenly powers,
one to another crying continually—
and we the while, weak and unworthy,
under their feet—

> *Holy, Holy, Holy,*
> *Lord God of Hosts;*
> *full is the whole heaven,*
> *and the whole earth,*
> *of the majesty of Thy glory. . . .* *

Jesus

---

* Fragment of the private written devotions of Lancelot Andrewes (1555-1626),
  chaplain to Queen Elizabeth I and one of the translators of the 1611 King James
  Version of the Bible

I Want to See You, Lord

One's ultimate loyalty must converge at a single point. To try to go two ways at once will rip a person down the middle.

—VERNARD ELLER

Jesus to Martha: "Only one thing is needed."

—LUKE 10:42

What is that one thing? Surely it is that God be loved and praised for Himself above all other occupations of the body or soul.

—THE CLOUD OF UNKNOWING

... Thee will I cherish,
Thee will I honor,
Thou, my soul's glory, joy and crown!

—"FAIREST LORD JESUS,"
SEVENTEENTH CENTURY HYMN

I Want to See You, Lord

The secret of successful Christians has
been that they had a sweet madness for
Jesus about them.

—A. W. Tozer

Jesus Christ is Square One, and anything
not related to Him is ultimately meaning-
less and futile.

—Unknown

Believers may not often realize it, but even
as believers we are either centered on God
or centered on man.

There is no alternative. Either God has become
the center of our universe and
we have become rightly adjusted to Him,
or we have made ourselves the center,
and are attempting to make everything else
orbit around us and for us.

—Paul Fromke

Dr. Henry Drummond to his theological
students: "Don't touch Christianity unless
you plan to make Him first. If you put
Him second, I promise you a miserable
existence."

Lord, Thou hast made us for Thyself, and
our hearts are restless until they rest in
Thee.

—St. Augustine,
FOURTH-FIFTH CENTURY

I Want to See You, Lord

Were I possessor of the earth
And call'd the stars my own,
Without Thy graces and Thyself
I were a wretch undone.
Let others stretch their arms like seas
And grasp in all the shore:
Grant me the visits of Thy face,
And I desire no more.

(I copied this 1827 poem, which was embroidered,
framed, and hanging on a wall of Crathes Castle in
northern Scotland.)

Every day I see again that only You can
teach me to pray, only You can set my
heart at rest, only You can let me dwell in
Your presence.

No book, no idea, no concept or theory
will ever bring me close to You unless You
Yourself are the One who lets these instru-
ments become the way to You.

—HENRI J. M. NOUWEN

I lift up my eyes to you, to you whose
throne is in heaven.

—PSALM 123:1

As to other gods I am an atheist, but as to
God the Son who came forth from Him
and taught us these things, I worship and
adore Him.

—JUSTIN MARTYR,
SECOND CENTURY

I Want to See You, Lord

I am A and Z, the First and Last!

—Jesus Christ, Revelation 1:11 TLB

Glorious God,
It is the flame of my life to worship Thee,
    the crown and glory of my soul to adore
        Thee,
    heavenly pleasure to approach.

—Old Puritan prayer

Lift up your heart unto God, then, with a
meek and longing love; let there be but a
naked intent unto God alone.

—The Cloud of Unknowing

None other Lamb, none other Name,
    None other Hope in heaven or earth or sea,
None other Hiding Place from guilt and
    shame—
    None beside Thee!

—Christina Rossetti, 1830-1894

My eyes are fixed on you, O Sovereign
Lord.

—Psalm 141:8

STUDY GUIDE
FOR GROUP USE

SESSION 1: Chapters 1-2

1. Chapter 1: Describe in your own words the salvation process, whereby God is on one side and man on the other, and Christ bringing us to God. When and how did you come to Him?

2. Chapter 2: *A frank admission of need* is always God's "ticket of admission" to His solutions. Do you see anything on the list on page 18 that you need to be saved from? Do you want to add others?

3. Read Hebrews 12:1-3, and spend time in group prayer that this study may meet your personal needs and direct your life focuses truly to Jesus.

To prepare for Session 2, let each member of the group pick one or two chapters between 3 and 9 with which he/she can identify, and be ready to report on those chapters, hopefully with personal applications.

SESSION 2: Chapters 3-9, to get practical help

Bring a kitchen timer clock to help monitor the timing of the reports on chapters 3 to 9! (Have some fun with this, but still try to keep on schedule.)

Then spend time in prayer for specific solutions to those areas of need.

Similarly, to prepare for Session 3, let each member of the group pick one or two chapters between 10 and 15 with which he/she can identify, and be ready to report on those chapters, hopefully with personal applications.

SESSION 3: *Chapters 10-15, to reshape your life*

Bring the kitchen timer clock again to help monitor the timing of the reports on chapters 10-15!

Then spend time in prayer for specific solutions to those areas of need.

SESSION 4: *Chapter 17, Jesus as seen in the Bible*

1. Pages 114-17: Have members of the group read John 5:39 and Luke 24:25-27, 44-45. Then let several pray that their minds may be open to understand Christ as seen in the Scriptures.

Together, look at each of the passages quoted in Chapter 17, putting one finger on the Old Testament quotation and another finger on the New Testament identification of Christ. Think how, over a span of so many centuries, God bound His book together by the person of His Son!

Can you name other New Testament passages that identify Jesus in the Old Testament? (For instance, there are at least 11 in the Gospel of Matthew.)

2a. On pages 118-19, when you see descriptions of yourself in the New Testament verses, what descriptions do you see that need particular prayer and obedience to be fulfilled in you?

2b. How can you help fellow group members characteristics (such as through intercessory prayer and accountability)? Do some strategizing!

Pray together in unison the verses in the Psalms quoted in the chapter's closing prayer. Continue praying your own prayers in the light of these.

SESSION 5: Chapters 18-19, Son of Man and Son of God

1. Read through these two chapters, looking up each Scripture verse mentioned and reading it in full.

2. Read Philippians 2:5-11.

    a. Which descriptions allude to Christ's being fully man? Which descriptions allude to His being fully God?

    b. What difference should it make in your attitude and personality when you obey verse 5?

3. Read all of Colossians 1:13-20, partially quoted on page 131. Describe all that you see here of various facets of Jesus Christ.

4. Read the poems between and following these two chapters. Then spend time in group prayer worshiping Him for being the perfect God-Man.

SESSION 6: Chapters 20-21, Jesus the crucified and risen One

1. Chapter 20, *Jesus crucified*

Read Joshua 20:1-6, a wonderful provision for Old Testament justice.

How does this situation picture Jesus as the innocent victim?

How does it also picture Him as our place of refuge?

2. Chapter 21, *Jesus risen*

Were you most struck by the risen Christ's provision of presence, peace, purpose, or power? Why?

Spend a time in prayers of thanksgiving for all these aspects of Jesus.

SESSION 7: Chapters 22-24, Jesus the Eternal One, the coming Lord, and focusing on nothing else

1. Chapter 22, *Jesus, the Eternal One*

Jesus says in John 14:2 that He is preparing a place for us. How do the following references which mention a "place" help to describe what that place might be like?

>   Exodus 3:5, Joshua 5:15
>   Psalm 26:8
>   Psalm 32:7
>   Isaiah 66:1

2. Chapter 23, *Jesus the Returning Lord*

First John 2:28 says we prepare for Jesus' coming by *abiding in Him.* Practically, how can we do that, to make sure we're ready for Him?

3. Chapter 24, *focusing on Jesus and on nothing else*

If Hebrews 12:2 says to look *away* to Jesus, what do you think of in your own life that you need to *look away from* to see Him more clearly?

Spend time in prayer, asking Him that you may do this—that you may focus off of specific things in order to focus on Him.

To prepare for Session 8, let each member of the group pick one or two chapters between 25-30 of particular personal interest, and be ready to report on those chapters, hopefully with personal applications.

SESSION 8: *Chapters 25-30, Focusing on Jesus*

Bring back that kitchen timer clock to help monitor the timing of the reports on chapters 25-30.

Then spend time in prayer for specific applications.

SESSION 9: *Wrap-up and worship*

Include the kitchen timer clock again! And let the reports conclude 15 to 20 minutes before closing time.

Finish with group worship:

1. Read in unison the prayer on page 194.

2. Sing hymns and songs about Christ's holiness (Use songbooks, or sing songs that you know.)

3. Perhaps on your knees, be in prayerful worship as members of the group volunteer to read to the Lord favorite quotations from chapter 31, in any order.

4. Continue with free worship in prayer, adoring Him, describing Him back to Himself, quoting Scriptures about Him, or breaking into worship songs.

5. Conclude, if you know it, by singing the Doxology.

My prayer is that this will be a book not just for you to *read* but to *do!* I would love to hear how you have fixed your eyes on Jesus anew.

Love,
Anne Ortlund

Renewal Ministries
4500 Campus Dr., Suite 662
Newport Beach, CA 92660

BIBLIOGRAPHY

Buechner, Frederick, *The Faces of Jesus* (Riverwood Publ., 1974; Stearn/Harper and Row, 1989).

The Cloud of Unknowing, a version in modern English of a four-teenth-century classic (NY: Harper and Bros., 1948).

Dods, Marcus, *Christ and Man* (London: Hodder and Stoughton, 1909).

Eller, Vernard, *The Simple Life* (Grand Rapids: Wm. B. Eerdmans Publ., 1973).

Frances de Sales, *Introduction to a Devout Life* (Cleveland, NY: World Publ. Co., 1952).

Gold Dust, Charlotte Yonge, ed. NY: Grosset and Dunlap, 1900, 1903).

Harton, F. P., *The Elements of the Spiritual Life* (London: S.P.C.K., Holy Trinity Church, 1932, 1964).

Hession, Roy and Revel, *We Would See Jesus* (Fort Washington, PA: Christian Literature Crusade, Publ., 1958).

Hopkins, Evan, "Threefold Delivery," message printed in *Keswick's Authentic Voice,* Herbert F. Stevenson, ed. (London: Marshall, Morgan and Scott, 1959).

Job, Reuben P., and Norman Shawchuck, *A Guide to Prayer* (Nashville: The Upper Room Publ., 1983).

The Keswick Week, 1955 (London: Marshall, Morgan and Scott, 1955).

King, Guy H., *Brought In* (London: Marshall, Morgan and Scott, 1949).

Lancelot Andrewe's Private Devotions (Cleveland, NY: World Publ. Co., 1956).

Bibliography

Law, William, *A Serious Call to a Devout and Holy Life* (Philadelphia: Westminster Press, 1948).

Lewis, C.S., *The Screwtape Letters,* (Minneapolis: Augsburg Fortress Press, 1980).

Maclaren, Alexander, *Christ in the Heart* (NY: Funk and Wagnalis Publ., 1905).

Monod, Theodore, *Looking unto Jesus* (pamphlet tr. French to English by Helen Willis, printed in Hong Kong, 1957).

Murray, Andrew, *Abide in Christ* (NY: Grosset and Dunlap, undated).

Murray, Andrew, *Like Christ* (NY: Fleming H. Revell, 1895).

Ortlund, Anne, *Discipling One Another* (Dallas: Word Books, 1979).

Ortlund, Anne, *Up with Worship* (Ventura, CA: Regal Books, 1975, 1982).

Ortlund, Raymond C., *Lord, Make My Life a Miracle* (Ventura, CA: Regal Books, 1974).

The Pocket William Law, excerpts of writings c. 1750, Arthur W. Hopkinson, ed. (London: Latimer House Ltd., 1950).

Sanders, Oswald J, *Christ Incomparable* (Fort Washington, PA: Christian Literature Crusade Publ., 1952).

Still Waters, Deep Waters, Rowland Croucher, ed. (Sydney: Albatross Books, 1987).

Tozer, A.W., *The Pursuit of God* (Harrisburg, PA: Christian Publications, 1948).

The Valley of Vision, Arthur Bennett, ed. (Edinburgh: The Banner of Truth Trust, 1975).

NOTES

1. Oswald J. Sanders, *Christ Incomparable,* p. 167.
2. See my book *Discipling One Another* (Waco, TX: Word Books, 1979).
3. A.W. Tozer, *The Pursuit of God,* pp. 94-95.
4. *Up with Worship,* pp. 47-48.
5. Frances de Sales, *Introduction to a Devout Life,* pp. 298-99.
6. p. 151.
7. For more helps on private prayer and Bible reading, see my book *Disciplines of the Beautiful Woman,* pages 71-73 and 118-22.
8. If you're interested in acquiring a notebook, write me. Ray and I have put together for others, at minimum cost, the same kind of notebook that we use. Our address is at the end of the text of this book.
9. William Law, *A Serious Call to a Devout and Holy Life,* p. 155.
10. P. Doddridge, "Keswick Calendar," December 14, 1990.
11. William Law, *A Serious Call to a Devout and Holy Life,* p. 159.
12. Clifford Lewis, "Keswick Calendar," January 15, 1991.
13. Thomas Dorsey, 1938. Copyright 1938 Hill and Range Songs, Inc. Copyright received, assigned to Unichappell Music, Inc. (Rightson Music, publisher). Used by permission of Hal Leonard Corporation.
14. Matthew Bridges, "Crown Him with Many Crowns."
15. A.W. Tozer, *Still Waters, Deep Waters,* p. 66.
16. Ray and I suggest, as a guide, *The Daily Walk,* P.O. Box 478, Mt. Morris, IL 61054.
17. Oswald Sanders, *Christ Incomparable,* p. 33.
18. Ibid., pp. 43-44.
19. Fredrick Buechner, *The Faces of Jesus,* p. 23.
20. Ibid., p.172.
21. Lancelot Andrewes, quoted by Oswald Sanders, *Christ Incomparable,* p. 141.
22. Vernard Eller, *The Simple Life* (Grand Rapids: William B. Eerdmans Publ. Co., 1973), pp. 28-29.
23. Copyright 1922. Renewal 1950 by H.H. Lemmel. Assigned to Singspiration, Inc.
24. C.S. Lewis, *The Screwtape Letters* (Minneapolis: Augsburg Fortress Press, 1980).

OTHER BOOKS BY THE ORTLUNDS

ANNE ORTLUND

Up With Worship, Regal Books
Disciplines of the Beautiful Woman, Word Books
Discipling One Another, Word Books
Children are Wet Cement, Fleming H. Revell
Joanna: A Story of Renewal, Word Books
Building a Great Marriage, Fleming H. Revell
Disciplines of the Heart, Word Books
Disciplines of the Home, Word Books
My Sacrifice, His Fire, Word Books

RAYMOND C. AND ANNE ORTLUND

The Best Half of Life, Word Books
You Don't Have to Quit, Oliver-Nelson
Confident in Christ, Multnomah
Renewal, NavPress
A Man and His Loves, Word Books

RAYMOND C. ORTLUND

Be a New Christian All Your Life, Fleming H. Revell
Intersections, Word Books
Three Priorities for a Strong Local Church, Word Books
Lord, Make My Life a Miracle, Regal Books